Student Teams That Get RESULTS

Gayle H. **GREGORY** ▪ Lin **KUZMICH**

Student Teams That Get

RESULTS

Teaching Tools for the Differentiated Classroom

CORWIN
A SAGE Company

For information:

Corwin
A SAGE Company
2455 Teller Road
Thousand Oaks, California 91320
www.corwinpress.com

SAGE Ltd.
1 Oliver's Yard
55 City Road
London EC1Y 1SP
United Kingdom

SAGE India Pvt. Ltd.
B 1/I 1 Mohan Cooperative
   Industrial Area
Mathura Road, New Delhi
India 110 044

SAGE Asia-Pacific Pte. Ltd.
33 Pekin Street #02-01
Far East Square
Singapore 048763

Printed in the United States of America

Library of Congress Cataloging-in-Publication Data

Gregory, Gayle H.
Student teams that get results: teaching tools for the differentiated classroom/Gayle H. Gregory, Lin Kuzmich.
       p. cm.
Includes bibliographical references and index.
ISBN 978-1-4129-1701-8 (cloth)
ISBN 978-1-4129-1702-5 (pbk.)

   1. Active learning. 2. Teacher-student relationships. 3. Mixed ability grouping in education. I. Kuzmich, Lin. II. Title.

LB1027.27.G74 2010
371.3'6—dc22   2009037009

This book is printed on acid-free paper.

09 10 11 12 13 10 9 8 7 6 5 4 3 2 1

Acquisitions Editor:	Hudson Perigo
Associate Editor:	Julie McNall
Production Editor:	Libby Larson
Copy Editor:	Jeannette McCoy
Typesetter:	C&M Digitals (P) Ltd.
Proofreader:	Susan Schon
Indexer:	Terri Corry
Cover Designer:	Scott Van Atta
Graphic Designer:	Karine Hovespian

Contents

 Further resources related to *Student Teams That Get Results* can be found at www.CorwinPress.com/studentteams_resources

Acknowledgments

Gayle Gregory and Lin Kuzmich wish to thank the Corwin staff for their continued assistance and support of our publications. We learn from great professionals around the country dedicated to the success of all children. We want to return the favor by sharing what we have learned about students and improving achievement. Sharing, teaming, thinking, and hands-on meaningful learning is essential to student success. We appreciate the many fine authors and practitioners who have contributed to the field of student learning and growth.

Gayle and Lin work with dedicated teachers and leaders who are working hard to meet the needs of diverse learners. This book is designed to combine the need for students to work together and think critically about their own learning. Educators today face so many challenges; we hope this book provides many tools to help them accomplish great things for students. Educators are our heroes, and we hope their journey is successful for the sake of their students and for our future.

Gayle, Lin, and Corwin would like to thank the following people and organizations:

Gayle's and Lin's families for putting up with the authors and their ways.

Aikens Lake Wilderness Lodge, located near the inlet to the Gammon River in the Atikaki Wilderness Provincial Park in Manitoba, Canada, and their staff for creating Lin's ideal writing environment.

The folks at Thinking Maps, Inc. for letting us refer to their work—Thinking Maps.

Dinah Zike for her permission to refer to those incredible Foldables.

The International Center for Leadership in Education and their incredible work on the Rigor and Relevance Framework and learning strategies that helped inspire some of this work.

Art Costa and Bob Garmston for the inspiration and leadership in helping students think critically.

Pat Wolfe and Ron Brandt for informing our knowledge of the brain and learning.

Barbara Given whose work on the "Theaters of the Mind" is an inspiration to thousands of educators.

Gibbs, Johnson and Johnson, Slavin, and Kagan for all their excellent work on grouping and strategies for student interaction.

Bob Marzano who both of us regard as a friend and mentor.

About the Authors

 **Gayle H. Gregory** is an internationally known consultant who has specialized in brain compatible learning and differentiated instruction and assessment.

She presents practical teacher/student-friendly strategies grounded in sound research that educators find easy to use in the classroom or schoolhouse tomorrow. Her interactive style and modeling of strategies help teachers and administrators transfer new ideas with ease.

She has had extensive experience in elementary, middle, and secondary schools, and in community colleges and universities. Gayle has also had district leadership roles including curriculum coordinator and staff development director. She has worked with Instructional Leadership Teams in many schools and districts throughout the country focusing on data analysis; using assessment, both formative and summative; and differentiating instruction based on readiness, learning profiles and interests.

Her areas of expertise include brain-compatible learning, block scheduling, emotional intelligence, instructional and assessment practices, differentiated instructional strategies, using data to differentiate, literacy, presentation skills, renewal of secondary schools, enhancing teacher quality, coaching and mentoring, managing change, and building professional learning communities.

Gayle is affiliated with many organizations, including the Association for Supervision and Curriculum Development and the National Staff Development Council, and is the author and co-author of numerous publications for teachers and administrators.

Gayle believes in lifelong learning for herself and others.

Gayle may be contacted at 905-336-6565 or 716-898-8716, or gregorygayle@netscape.net. Her Web site is www.gaylehgregory.com

Lin Kuzmich is a consultant, adjunct professor, and author from Loveland, Colorado. She served Thompson School District as the assistant superintendent, executive director of secondary and elementary instruction, director of professional development, assistant director of special education, and as the building principal for nine years. Lin's school was named a 2000 winner of the John R. Irwin Award for Academic Excellence and Improvement. Lin has taught elementary, middle, and high school levels in both regular and special education. Lin earned the Teacher of the Year Award for Denver Public Schools in 1979 and was Northern Colorado Principal of the Year in 2000. In addition, for the past decade, she was involved in staff development through several universities and the Tointon Institute for Educational Change. Currently, Lin is an adjunct professor/instructor at Colorado State University in the Principal Preparation Program. She is a Senior Consultant for the International Center for Leadership in Education. Lin is affiliated with many organizations, including the Association for Supervision and Curriculum Development and the National Association of Secondary Principals, and presents at numerous national conferences. Lin currently works with schools and districts across the country that are struggling to meet the needs of diverse learners, the requirements of state and national laws, and the changing education practices needed for the future success of our students. Lin's work with schools improves achievement results for students and increases the capacity of staff. Lin is passionate about helping educators prepare today's students for a successful future. Lin can be reached at 970-669-2290 or kuzenergy@gmail.com. Her Web site is www.kcsink.org.

Gayle Gregory's National Publications

Designing Brain-Compatible Learning, Second Edition

Thinking Inside the Block Schedule: Strategies for Teaching in Extended Periods of Time

Differentiated Instructional Strategies: One Size Doesn't Fit All, Second Edition

Differentiated Instructional Strategies in Practice: Training, Implementation, and Supervision

Differentiation With Style to Maximize Student Achievement

Differentiated Instructional Strategies for Science

Videos:

Gayle is featured in the Video Journal of Education's bestselling elementary and secondary videos, *Differentiating Instruction to Meet the Needs of All Learners.*

Lin Kuzmich's Government and National Publications

Published by Colorado Department of Education and the Centennial BOCES:

School Improvement Planning

Data Driven Instruction Kit and video

Facilitating Evaluation in a Standards-Based Classroom

Published by International Center for Leadership in Education (Rexford, NY):

Redefining Literacy in Grades 7–12: Strategies for Document, Technological, and Quantitative Literacy

21st Century Learning Criteria: Stretch Learning (Upcoming publication winter 2009)

Gayle and Lin's Joint National Publications

Data Driven Differentiation in the Standards-Based Classroom

Differentiated Literacy Strategies for Student Growth Grades K–6

Differentiated Literacy Strategies for Student Growth Grades 7–12

The Differentiated Instructional Strategies 10 Book Collection

Teacher Teams That Get Results

Teacher Teams That Get Results Multimedia Kit

Gayle and Lin are featured in the Video Journal of Education's elementary and secondary video: *Applied Differentiation: Making It Work in the Classroom.*

This book is dedicated to the memory of those we lost who inspired and loved us. Their loving memory lives on through our work and lives.

Joe Pavelka
Dorothy and Michael Gregory
Pat and Libby Horenstein
Steve and Catherine Kuzmich

1

Introduction to *Student Teams That Get Results*

> Why are connections essential? The essence of human interaction is social, based on relationships to create fertile soil for learning. Teachers and students must make daily and positive connections.
>
> Gregory and Kuzmich, 2004.

PURPOSE FOR THIS BOOK ■

Busy teachers struggle daily with the demands of increased accountability and need to develop skill and proficiency in diverse learners. Teachers want students to succeed and excel. We want to provide teachers with tools that make a difference and have high payoff in terms of results. Supplying teachers with high quality tools will help them increase student performance. Some tools work better than others and get results faster for many types of learners. Carefully chosen, brain-compatible and research-based tools help students deepen thinking and accelerate learning. Tools that actively engage students and connect to their emotional needs help busy teachers meet diverse learning needs. In this book, we focus on the power of collaboration and dialogue to serve diverse learners in a differentiated classroom. In a differentiated classroom, we rely on students' ability to work in flexible groups (partners or small groups). In these groups, we want to foster meaningful dialogue that deepens student understanding and facilitates aural and interactive rehearsal. Learning floats on a sea of conversation. Dialogue between and among learners is more powerful than a teacher talking to one student while the rest listen. The more minds that are engaged the better, and "it's hard to get left out of a pair" (Johnson & Johnson, 1991). Having to express ideas to others deepens understanding of concepts and clarifies thinking. Auditory learners benefit not only from the sound of the teacher's voice but also their peer's and their own voices. For teachers who are "eavesdropping," it's a great assessment tool. Just listening as students share ideas and explanations, teachers garner assessment data answering questions such as the following:

- Do they understand this material?
- Are there any misconceptions?
- Are there any gaps that need to be filled?
- How might I group students to capitalize on their knowledge and skill?

■ USING WHAT WE KNOW ABOUT THE BRAIN

Theaters of the Mind

Using the "Theaters of the Mind" helps teachers tap into the brain's five natural learning systems (Given, 2002a). This information about the brain helps us increase student transfer of learning and skills to successful performance. Each of our diverse learners in the differentiated classroom will benefit from opening the "cineplex" and using each theater to experience and process new information and skills.

Social Learning System

"All of us prefer to interact with those whose presence increases the brain's feel-good neurotransmitter brain levels, resulting from feelings of comfort, trust, respect, and affection" (Panksepp, 1998). Students benefit from frequent well planned social interaction in the classroom using techniques that foster a positive environment and deepens thinking. Examples of tools that support social learning include: organizers for decision making and problem solving, organizers that require cooperative group work to complete, and strategies that support the understanding of controversial social or political topics.

Emotional Learning System

People need to feel safe and supported to take risks. Students also need challenging tasks with a minimal level of threat or risk in order to learn new skills. Examples of strategies that support emotional learning include: methods that establish relevancy and access prior knowledge and organizers that require students to self evaluate thinking. Building a safe, supportive environment in a differentiated classroom helps all learners lower stress levels and recognize that we are more similar than different, but each of us have different strengths and needs. At times, a student or group of students will take the lead and other times follow. Fair isn't always equal and equal isn't always fair. Emotions play a large role in engaging attention. Brains like to enjoy themselves in the learning process. Why not make learning positive and fun (focused on learning goals of course) rather than stressful and threatening? Neurotransmitters are released in the brain during "eustress" (positive) that actually help in cementing information in long-term memory. It has been said that angels can fly because they take themselves lightly.

Cognitive Learning System

Conscious language development and focused attention increases memory. Students need to use all senses to process new information. Examples of advanced organizers that support cognitive learning include: organizers that help students see patterns, deepen concepts, and note relationships as well as organizers that connect new learning to prior background knowledge.

Physical Learning System

Active problem solving supports our physical needs. Interaction, movement, and creation of products are ways to develop a problem solving orientation to learning. Examples of advanced organizers that support physical learning include: organizers that are graphic and highly visual, require active engagement, and challenge established ideas or provide novelty. Physical movement lowers the cortisol and sodium levels that increase during stress. If these are continually in the blood stream over time, they can lower immunity and create barriers to learning. Movement pumps glucose and oxygen to the brain. Both are needed to keep the brain engaged and processing.

Reflective Learning System

Metacognition, questioning, analysis, reaction, and goal setting all help us reflect on what we do and the results we get. We will not be able to sustain new learning without this type of reflective practice and dialogue. Examples of advanced organizers that support reflective learning include: organizers that help students see their work in relationship to a criteria or model and include ways to apply and integrate learning, and organizers that help us use adaptive and analytic reasoning with future or unknown situations and applications of learning. We learn from experience if we reflect on experience.

Teachers fostering differentiation, who tap into all five "theaters of the mind," engage more diverse learners and increase the active processing and deeper understanding of new information and skills in a variety of ways.

BRAIN BITS   ■

Over the past twenty years, the emerging research and findings on how the brain operates has caused us to rethink student learning. The most important aspect of this research is how teachers use brain-friendly strategies tied to the desired results for learning.

Certain factors help us meet and support the brain based learning needs of students:

1. Students need to feel safe: students learn more and faster in trustworthy environments. Tools that provide risk free rehearsal and opportunities to celebrate help students feel safe.

2. Students need to learn in a state of relaxed alertness: students need high expectations with adequate support, encouragement, and feedback. Tools that develop routines and habits that have multiple applications help students anticipate learning in a relaxed manner.

3. Students need learning that allows an emotional impact: students need a personal connection, need to satisfy an urge "to know," and know that their learning makes a difference. Tools that connect to students' prior knowledge and are engaging or challenging help students make emotional connections.

4. Students need social relationships: learners crave validation and acceptance from peers and teachers. Tools that help students work in various size groups support this tendency.

5. Students need to form patterns, seek meaning and relevancy, and set goals: students need to connect prior knowledge and experience to new ideas and to integrate the new learning with the old. Tools that are graphic, seek to show relationships, and are relevant support student needs to form meaning.

6. Students enjoy an active learning environment that is engaging: students need to construct their own meaning from new knowledge and skills in a form that makes sense. Tools that encourage inference, creativity, and adaptive reasoning help students deepen understanding and increase lifelong learning.

7. Students need learning that supports multiple pathways to memory: students need variety and multi-sensory approaches to meet individual processing and learning needs. Tools that work with student learning styles and methods of knowing help increase long-term memory.

The brain's job in the first five to seven years is to get upright, mobile, and communicate. Communication begins with the spoken word. This ability is hard-wired in the brain. A child immersed in any culture will pick up the spoken word with no formal training.

■ USING WHAT WE KNOW ABOUT RESEARCH-BASED PRACTICES

Marzano, Pickering, and Pollack (2001) detail the research and effect size that clearly indicates the usefulness and success of such tools as questioning, using advanced organizers, note taking strategies, etc. There are certainly many types of tools and in this book we use brain-friendly methods, strategies that help teachers meet diverse learners' styles of learning, and tools that are research-based.

The following figure connects the instructional strategies research to what we know about the brain and then offers tactics to use every day in the classroom.

Classroom Instruction That Works Tied to Brain Research

Instructional Strategies	Percentile Gain	Brain Research	Tactics
Similarities and differences, compare, contrast, classifying, analogies and metaphors	45	**Brain seeks patterns, connections, and relationships between and among prior and new learning.**	**Classifying Compare, contrast Venn Synectics Concept attainment Concept formation iREAP T and Y charts**
Note taking and summarizing	34	**The brain pays attention to meaningful information and deletes that which is not relevant.**	**Mind maps Word webs Jigsaw Reciprocal teaching Four-corner processing Point of View iREAP**
Reinforcing effort and providing recognition	29	**Brain responds to challenge and not to threat. Emotions enhance learning.**	**Stories of determination Celebrate successes**
Assigning homework and practice	28	**If you don't use it, you lose it. Practice and rehearsal makes learning "stick."**	**Create challenges in a variety of ways**
Generating nonlinguistic representations	27	**The brain is a parallel processor. Visual stimuli are recalled with 90% accuracy.**	**Mind maps Graphic organizers Models Wallpaper Poster**
Using Cooperative Group Learning	27	**The brain is social. Collaboration facilitates understanding and higher order thinking.**	**Think-Pair-Share Say and Switch ABC Conversations Random Partners Jigsaw P.I.G.S.F. Community Circle Give and Go**
Setting objectives and providing feedback	23	**The brain responds to high challenge and continues to strive based on feedback.**	**Helpful feedback Rubrics Criteria Expectations Right angle**
Generating and testing hypothesis	23	**The brain is curious and has an innate need to make meaning through patterns.**	**Problem based/Inquiry Portfolios Case studies Question matters Cause and Effect**
Providing questions, cues, and advance organizers	22	**The brain responds to wholes and parts. All learners need to open "mental files" into which new learning can be hooked.**	**Wait time Questioning techniques Agenda maps Cubing Question matters**

SOURCE: Adapted from: Marzano, R., Pickering, D., & Pollack, J. (2001) and Gregory, G., & Parry, T. (2006)

This book will deal with several of the McREL strategies that teachers can use easily with very little preparation time and effort. One of the primary functions of this book is to help teachers take cooperative group learning to new levels when paired with other effective critical thinking strategies such as graphic organizers, appropriate note taking, and other tools to increase thinking skills within group learning. It might be said that if every classroom teacher had these nine strategies in executive control, we might be differentiating enough—as they attend to the various learning styles and multiple intelligences of diverse learners. They also provide a great variety of tools in the "toolkit" for differentiating instruction.

Cooperative group learning research for the last 25 years suggests that when group learning is implemented effectively, we can expect our students to have the following (adapted from Johnson, Johnson, & Holubec, 1993):

- High self-esteem
- Higher achievement
- Increased retention
- Greater social support
- More on-task behavior
- Greater collaborative skills
- Greater intrinsic motivation
- Increased perspective taking
- Better attitudes toward school
- Better attitudes toward teachers
- Greater use of high level reasoning
- More positive psychological adjustment

The clear benefits to students are well documented. The key is to make certain that group work is high quality, not just a place to get help filling out a worksheet. By pairing great grouping strategies with other practices, which increase student achievement, this book is designed to help teachers select quality methods of raising achievement and critical thinking for all students in a differentiated classroom.

Three top skills students need to work in a group:

1. Attentive Listening
   - Check for understanding: Do you mean . . . ? I think I heard you say . . . .
   - Body language speaks volumes; learn to read it in others.

2. Accepting Others' Ideas
   - Thank group members.
   - Give feedback.
   - Celebrate.

3. Disagreeing With Ideas, Not People
   - Use I statements . . . .
   - Your idea is interesting, *and* I think . . . .

In order to actively construct meaning, students need tools to organize information and skills, develop patterns that can be retrieved by the brain from multiple pathways, and connect personally with the relevance of the learning or skill acquisition. Choosing the right strategies helps us deepen thinking and increase the probability that students can use this to adapt to unknown future circumstances like advanced classes, employment possibilities, and successful social and community interactions. We know that graphic organizers and visual representations are powerful research-based strategies with huge effects on raising achievement results. In this book, many of our collaboration strategies are paired with graphic organizers and visual representations. Given a generation that is exposed to multiple visual stimuli and extensive social networking, these strategies match their brains' natural tendencies.

Tools that improve thinking by their nature can be used ahead of a formative or summative assessment. Data-driven instructional choices have two paths to successful student growth. You can plan strategies for teaching and learning based on what students know and can do now, and you can plan based on what you want students to know and be able to do at the end of a unit, class, or period of time, thus differentiating. Planning from what students can do now works great for continuous progress subjects like learning to read and write. Planning backward from where students need to be is a powerful way to accelerate learning and increase the potential of more students demonstrating proficient or higher levels of performance (Gregory & Kuzmich, 2004). The tools in this book are designed to help support your backward design from a summative or formative assessment and therefore increase student achievement through planning for differentiation.

USING WHAT WE KNOW ABOUT STUDENTS AND LEARNING STYLES

The tools in this book also appeal to the diverse learning styles represented in our students. We use analogous thinking to represent the four styles as the everyday item associated with the particular style also gives the attributes of that style.

Puppy as the Interpersonal Learner (Abstract Random)

These learners like to interact with other learners, discuss, socialize, and thrive on teacher approval and nurturing. They want teachers to make the learning relevant to them so that the learning is personalized and meaningful. They like cooperative groups and partner work in a supportive enabling environment.

Microscope as the Analytical Learner (Abstract Sequential)

These learners like to analyze, compare, contrast, classify, and summarize their learning. They appreciate quality information and then a chance to digest, probe, and think logically and analytically. They like to work alone and do in-depth study of things that interest and challenge them. They often think group work is "pooled ignorance" and would rather have a good lecture.

Clipboard as the Sequential Learner (Concrete Sequential)

These learners like to practice, observe, describe, and memorize new learning to be successful. They like information presented to them and like to "practice 'til perfect." They appreciate order, routine, and "no surprises."

Beach Ball as the Expressive Learner (Concrete Random)

These learners like originality, spontaneity, and elaborative thinking. They like choices and are creative, innovative learners. They are bored always doing the same thing and think "variety is the spice of life."

The variety of tools provided will appeal to multiple styles with organizational strengths, interpersonal opportunities, investigative aspects, and creative vestiges. Some of the preferences for the four learning styles are shown in this figure.

Learning Styles

The Beach Ball Learner prefers	**The Puppy Learner prefers**
PMI Star gazing Four Squares for Creativity Exhibitions Presentations Hypothesizing Research Predictions Investigation Collaborative products Innovations	People Search Sharing standards & purpose Agenda K.W.L. Think-Pair-Share Mind maps Four-corner graphic Group graffiti Ticket Out Journal entry Survey 
The Clipboard Learner prefers	**The Microscope Learner prefers**
Practice, rehearsal Fishbone Prioritizing Note taking and summarizing Graphic organizers Labs Quizzes Demonstrations Projects Problem-based Centers	Graphic organizers Points of view Lecturette Video Internet search Software, CD Text Independent reading Resource books Audio tape Guest speaker Field trip 

SOURCE: Gregory and Kuzmich (2004)

With a variety of learner preferences in a differentiated classroom, it is important to provide for all four continually. It is not the intent to label the learner and cater to the preference but to recognize that we have the diversity of preferences and continue to ask the question as reflective practitioners: *What is there in this learning experience that will attend to and satisfy each style?* For example, there should be clear directions and expectations for the clipboard, opportunities to interact with others for the puppy, analytical thinking and investigation for the microscope, and choice to satisfy the beach ball.

REHEARSAL TO GET TO LONG-TERM MEMORY ■

Information first comes into the brain through sensory stimuli. If the information captures our attention, it will be moved to short-term memory. If we want to retain that information or develop the skill, we need to rehearse it in our working memory such that it can be processed by the hippocampus and filed in long-term memory. The tools in this book are appropriate ways to process and rehearse information and skills so that it makes the leap into long-term storage and can be retrieved when needed on tests or for life.

It is one thing to remember and yet another to do something with that memory. Once in long-term memory, we can retrieve the information, integrate it, and use it in relevant ways to solve problems, design solutions, and create your life.

The challenge for teachers in a differentiated classroom is that each student's sensory memory responds or engages in a variety of unique ways through relevance, novelty, or meaning. Also, in the rehearsal or working memory phase, different learners prefer different modes. Since some learners need more rehearsals, we need a variety of ways to both engage learners and sustain the interest level during multiple focused practices. We've learned over the years that "louder and slower from another part of the room" isn't the best second strategy. Thus, in this book, we are providing numerous ways for students to actively process new skill and information.

BENEFITS OF USING THESE TOOLS ■
AND GETTING THE INTENDED RESULTS

Strategies that provide students with "cognitive structures so that they have 'mental hooks' on which to 'hang' new concepts and information from . . . learning" get better and more rapid results (Robbins, Gregory, & Herndon, 2000). Students will demonstrate increased proficiency on future assessments if teachers provide the tools that help students' rehearsal for the type of required thinking and skill demonstration. In order to prepare students for deeper and more successful thinking on assessments, teachers need tools that help students:

- Scaffold critical layers of meaning
- Generalize and infer
- Integrate content

- Identify patterns
- Increase adaptive and analytic reasoning

. . . the brain is essentially curious and it must be to survive. It constantly seeks connections between the new and the known. Learning is a process of active construction by the learner. (Wolfe & Brandt, 1998, p. 11)

■ IN THIS BOOK: TOOLS THAT GET RESULTS

We have organized this book into three sections that reflect aspects of learning that develop comprehension, deepen thinking through application, and provide tools for differentiating instruction.

Teaming to Learn: The number one reason people lose their jobs is surprising. It is not because they don't know or can't do. It's because they can't work together to accomplish what the organization needs. Though we don't know the needs of the future workplace, we do know you will still need to collaborate with colleagues—virtually or face to face. Thus we must give students the opportunity to work productively together to accomplish tasks and deepen learning. In these processes, we need to overtly teach social skills that they need for life.

Sharing Knowledge and Skills: The brain needs multiple rehearsals to reach long-term memory. Transferring and strengthening understanding requires learning through many pathways. We learn more deeply that which we can explain, teach, or demonstrate.

Integrating and Applying Knowledge: Relevant application of learning helps students deepen understanding. Tasks that allow students to use what they have acquired in motivating ways allow learning to "stick." When learning sticks, students achieve more, test with better results, and have access to more options and opportunities for higher-level classes and post-secondary education.

Student Teams That Get Results

Teaming to Learn	Sharing Knowledge and Skills	Integrating and Applying Learning
Purpose: Learning routines Understanding roles Developing team Celebrating success Getting and giving feedback Communicating Building trust Peer coaching Team process evaluation	Purpose: Learning content Developing understanding Developing learning strategies Developing schema Learning multiple routines Transferring Expanding options Sharing Peer support	Purpose: Learning to use knowledge Goal setting Long-term memory Developing generalization Generating hypotheses Critical thinking skills Analysis skills Problem-solving strategies Developing creativity Successful teamwork
1. Community Circle 2. Find Some Who 3. Four-Corner Cards 4. Random Partners 5. T-Chart and Y-Chart 6. Graffiti 7. Think-Pair-Share and Say and Switch	8. ABC Conversations 9. 3-2-1 with Consulting Line or Inside-Outside Circles 10. Jigsaw Methods 11. Concept Formation 12. Content Dialogue 13. Note Taking and Summarizing 14. Wallpaper Poster	15. Four Squares for Creativity 16. Point of View 17. iREAP 18. Question Cubing 19. Cause and Effect 20. Right Angle 21. Synectics

We hope you use the strategies in this book in combination or alone. Use these strategies to deepen understanding, better retain new learning, and to increase content-based dialogue. Use these strategies to strengthen relationships. Without relationships, there is no learning.

Student learning and growth is too critical to leave to chance. Random use of good strategies is not nearly as beneficial as tying the selection of the tool to the intended result. A doctor does not randomly choose medication; instead, given the data and the desired result, he or she carefully selects the right remedy. A busy teacher committed to student learning also needs to choose the right tools for teaching and learning tied to what is known about learners and for the next levels of desired growth and achievement.

2

Teaming to Learn

Introduction

A positive learning climate in any classroom but certainly in a differentiated one is essential for all learners to succeed. It is the inclusive, supportive climate that allows for relaxed alertness and optimal learning.

Teachers create a culture for learning that is represented by the following conditions:

- Supportive
- Safe
- Inclusive
- Nonthreatening
- Free of blame and negativity
- Enabling
- Enthusiastic
- Trusting

- Open so learners can take risks without fear
- Sharing and problem solving
- Accepting of challenges

The learning atmosphere is pervasive and speaks through words, actions, and subtleties. The culture may be labeled as toxic, positive, negative, or enabling. If a positive, enabling atmosphere is not present, learners do not thrive. The climate will not be growth oriented. The classroom needs to be such that all students can learn and grow together, whatever their age. A growth-oriented climate results when these conditions exist.

The following chart suggests positive and negative indicators of climate.

Positive	Negative
Encouraging atmosphere	Toxic culture
Choices and variety	Unnecessary pressure
Appropriate time provided	Unrealistic time frames
Constructive feedback offered	Little or no feedback
Safety ensured	Inappropriate challenges
"Relaxed alertness" ensured	Uneasiness related to expectations
Helpful support and encouragement	Critical and judgmental environment
Personality styles honored	Individual needs ignored

A positive climate is built on trust. When we engage in group activities, comfort comes from knowledge of one another and trust that grows over time. Trust develops through positive interaction fostered by formal and informal teacher leadership.

◼ EMOTIONAL INTELLIGENCE

Daniel Goleman (1995) suggests that there are five domains that constitute emotional intelligence:

- Self-awareness of emotions: Self-awareness is one's ability to sense and name a feeling when it happens and also to put it into words. Self-aware people can use appropriate strategies to deal with their moods by sharing frustrations with others or seeking support on a bad day.
- Managing emotions: Managing emotions is an outcome of recognizing and labeling feelings. It is the ability to calm and soothe during anxious moments or to manage and deal with anger.
- Self-motivation: Self-motivation consists of competencies such as persistence, setting one's own goals, and delaying gratification.
- Empathy: empathy is being able to feel for another.
- Social skills: Social skills are the competencies that one uses to "read" other people and manage emotional interactions. People with high levels of social competencies have the ability to handle relationships well and are able to adapt to a variety of social situations. Goleman

(1995) suggests this is a key skill in life, and employers see it as essential in a 21st century employee.

This is supported from multiple sources. In the United States Department of Labor report from the Secretary's Commission on Achieving Necessary Skills (SCANS) (see http://wdr.doleta.gov/SCANS/) the following is provided:

SCANS: A Three-Part Foundation

Basic Skills: Reads, writes, performs arithmetic and mathematical operations, listens, and speaks.

1. Reading: Locates, understands, and interprets written information in prose and in documents such as manuals, graphs, and schedules.

2. Writing: Communicates thoughts, ideas, information, and messages in writing and creates documents such as letters, directions, manuals, reports, graphs, and flow charts.

3. Arithmetic: Performs basic computations and approaches practical problems by choosing appropriately from a variety of mathematical techniques.

4. Listening: Receives, attends to, interprets, and responds to verbal messages and other cues.

5. Speaking: Organizes ideas and communicates orally.

Thinking Skills: Thinks creatively, makes decisions, solves problems, visualizes, knows how to learn, and reasons.

1. Creative Thinking: Generates new ideas.

2. Decision Making: Specifies goals and constraints, generates alternatives, considers risks, and evaluates and chooses best alternative.

3. Problem Solving: Recognizes problems and devises and implements plan of action.

4. Seeing Things in the Mind's Eye: Organizes and processes symbols, pictures, graphs, objects, and other information.

5. Knowing How to Learn: Uses efficient learning techniques to acquire and apply new knowledge and skills.

6. Reasoning: Discovers a rule or principle underlying the relationship between two or more objects and applies it when solving a problem.

Personal Qualities: Displays responsibility, self-esteem, sociability, self-management, and integrity and honesty.

1. Responsibility: Exerts a high level of effort and perseveres toward goal attainment.

2. Self-Esteem: Believes in own self-worth and maintains a positive view of self.

3. Sociability: Demonstrates understanding, friendliness, adaptability, empathy, and politeness in group settings.

4. Self-Management: Assesses self-accurately, sets personal goals, monitors progress, and exhibits self-control.

5. Integrity and Honesty: Chooses ethical courses of action.

The Conference Board of Canada Employability Skills (see http://www.conferenceboard.ca/topics/education) also suggests the following:

Fundamental Skills	Personal Management Skills	Teamwork Skills
The skills needed as a base for further development.	The personal skills, attitudes, and behaviors that drive one's potential for growth.	The skills and attitudes needed to contribute productively.
✓ Communication ✓ Managing Information ✓ Using numbers ✓ Thinking and solving problems	✓ Demonstrate positive attitudes and behaviors ✓ Be responsible ✓ Be adaptable ✓ Learn continually ✓ Work safely	✓ Working with others ✓ Participating in projects

Both skill sets include a variety of skills students need for life. We are fostering social interaction, thinking, and problem solving in the classroom so as not only to prepare them for "the standardized test" but also for a successful life. Many students lack social skills, as they have spent many hours in front of screens, both television and computers, and are not necessarily learning how to interact with others in a positive way. We develop social skills by being in social situations and practicing positive ways of interacting. Watching inappropriate media and not having positive opportunities with others interfere with a young person's development of social skills.

■ VALUING TEAMING

Trust and respect are key components for a successful learning community to thrive. In a differentiated classroom, each student has had a different background and experiences. Students also have different preferences and strengths in multiple intelligences that tend to be complementary as they work together. It is important that students honor those differences and appreciate how they bring greater depth and capability to the interactions in the classroom. The more students feel valued, the more they tend to continue to contribute and receive feelings of self-worth and self-confidence.

Here are some examples of rewards you can give as these critical skills emerge.

Creativity Award

This award is given to

_____

For helping us to

_____

_____

Date: _____

To the Rescue

This award is given to

_____

for helping _____to

_____

_____

Date: _____

Possibility Thinking...

This award is given to

_____

For

_____ to

_____

_____

Date: _____

Action Oriented

This award is given to

_____

For helping us

_____

_____

_____

Date: _____

Giving the Rose...

This award is given to

_____

For

_____

_____

_____

Date: _____

PURPOSEFUL TEAMING   ■

David Conley's (2007) research on college and post-secondary readiness is an eye-opening piece to think about as we approach purposeful teaming. Conley found four key factors for readiness and success in post-secondary education:

1. cognitive strategies,

2. content knowledge,

3. self-management skills,

4. knowledge about post-secondary education.

Key cognitive strategies include a student's ability to

- think about the current learning,
- make connections,
- evaluate,
- analyze,
- use logic and other higher level
- cognitive strategies.

In this book, we provide some practical pieces for getting started in this section on teaming to learn, then increase the cognitive demands in the section on sharing knowledge and skills, and then really integrate the highest levels of thinking in the last section on integrating and applying learning.

In terms of Conley's thinking on self-management, a key factor is knowing you need help, seeking that help, and participating with others to study and learn. In this section of the book are strategies to help students get those self-management skills for group study to a purposeful and useful level.

We used these criteria as we selected and developed the strategies in this section of the book. We feel strongly that a well-rehearsed process and communication are worth the time spent teaching and practicing, and these should be reviewed with each grouping opportunity. By paying close attention to the following criteria for successful cooperative groups, we can achieve higher functioning teams that contribute to each other's learning:

- Demonstrate the learning of routines
- Develop understanding and demonstrate group roles
- Participate and contribute to the development of the team
- Practice celebrating success of the group
- Give great feedback and self-evaluate contributions to the team and learning
- Demonstrate effective communication skills
- Contribute toward actions and practices that build trust
- Provide peer coaching and support
- Evaluate the effectiveness of the team given the learning purpose and results

We hope you find these teaming strategies effectively build teams that are ready to learn and contribute to each other's success. These skills open up options and opportunities for students now and in the future.

TEAMING TO LEARN
Community Circle

PURPOSE AND DESCRIPTION ■

A safe, connected community circle allows participants to feel included and have a voice and creates a positive climate. It is a vehicle for sharing, reflecting, discussing, and celebrating.

Making Connections

Brain Bits	This process emphasizes the Reflective Learning system; students think more critically and creatively when given the opportunity to question and analyze a topic deeply. This process supports social and active learning and gives students access to new ideas and to integrate the new learning with the old. Also, it provides cognitive rehearsal, including the development of vocabulary, clarifying, and sharing.
Theaters of the Mind	Emotional, Social, Physical, Reflective, and Cognitive Learning.
Learning Styles	Beach Ball: creative and random, Puppy: processing, Clipboard: orderly process, Microscope: analytical
Research Basis	Questioning, cues and advanced organizers, nonlinguistic representation, using similarities and differences, analogies and metaphors, summarizing and note taking, cooperative learning, generating hypothesis, and cognitive complexity are all utilized.
Grouping	Use with groups of any number students in the circle depending on space available. May have more than one circle at a time to save time.
Grade Level	This technique works for late elementary, middle level, and high school. For younger or less-literate students, this could be used as a whole-group discussion tool to model this type of thinking.
Timing	This takes 10 to 20 minutes with prior modeling by the teacher. Use with very small groups toward the end of the unit or for a formative assessment during the unit.
Other Notes	Ask questions during group processing to support originality and creativity. *What if . . . ? How could we . . . ? Why not . . . ?* and so on all work well to enhance thinking.

STEPS AND DIRECTIONS

Ask participants to bring chairs and sit in a circle where everyone can see everyone. (Chairs may be set up previously or a carpeted area could be used so students can sit on the floor.)

1. A prompt or question is posed and students are given time to think of a response.

2. Invite a volunteer to start.

3. Go around the circle—each person speaks in turn.

4. If someone is not ready to share or needs a little more think time, Right to Pass may be used. The person will say, "Pass," and then the teacher will move on to the next person. People who pass will be asked to respond later.

■ OTHER NOTES

This can be used for the following conditions:

- For students to share ideas that the whole group can see and hear
- To celebrate things that have been accomplished
- To discuss ideas and have students develop listening skills in a supportive environment

Examples and Uses

1. At the end of a class, each student in the circle may give a thank you or a compliment to someone in the class for his or her help, good idea, or kindness that day.

2. One idea may be to share opinions about an issue. Each student in turn gives a perspective or point of view concerning the issue at the beginning of a topic or at the end of the session to consolidate or bring the discussion to a conclusion.

3. Students can form a community circle in order to process ideas during a class discussion so that each student is on equal footing and can make eye contact with everyone in the group.

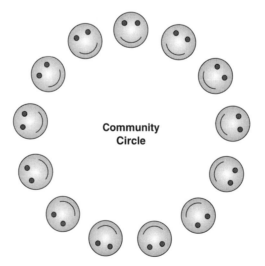

Community
Circle

■ SELECTED REFERENCES

Australian Government Department of Education (2006), Chadwick (2006), Gibbs (2001).

TEAMING TO LEARN
Find Someone Who

PURPOSE AND DESCRIPTION ■

Find Someone Who . . . or the *People Search* can be used as a getting-to-know-you activity or an ice breaker. It can be used with personal information or instructional material that students need to dialogue about, review, or check for clarification.

Making Connections

Brain Bits	Seek meaning, relevancy, and connections
Theaters of the Mind	Reflective Learning
Learning Styles	Microscope: visual learning
Research Basis	Questioning, cues and advanced organizers, homework
Grouping	Use with one, two, or three student groups.
Grade Level	This technique works for late elementary, middle level, and high school.
Timing	Use individually toward the end of the unit or for a formative assessment during the unit. Use as an assignment or for homework with two or three students at the beginning or middle of the unit.
Other Notes	Ask questions during group processing to support checking assumptions, author's point of view, and inferential thinking.

STEPS AND DIRECTIONS

1. Give students a bingo grid or list of items for which they need to find someone to answer or give them information.

2. Each student takes his or her list and walks around the room trying to find someone who is able to give an answer to a question on the sheet.

3. The student listens attentively to the answer that is given and jots down the name of the person who answered the question beside the question.

4. When all students have completed their grid, students can report what they have heard and learned from others.

■ OTHER NOTES

This can be used for the following conditions:

- Students need some active involvement related to developing connections and relationships with others in the classroom
- Anytime students need a change of state and another student to discuss an idea
- Students need to move or get up
- The teacher wants to lower the risk for participation
- There is a need for team building
- Content needs to be shared and discussed or assessed and reviewed

Example and Uses

A. Early Elementary Example: Students are comparing and contrasting folk tales.

■ FIND SOMEONE WHO . . .

1. Can explain why the wicked fairy put a spell on Sleeping Beauty _____

2. Can say what was similar in the *Three Little Pigs* and *Goldilocks and the Three Bears* _____

3. Can tell what Jack used the money for in *Jack and the Beanstalk* _____

4. Can explain why Red Riding Hood was in danger _____

5. Can tell how the prince found Cinderella _____

B. Middle School Example: People Searches can also be done on a Bingo card.

FIND SOMEONE WHO . . . ■

Can give one example of a way to solve a problem	Can explain why problem solving is an important skill to learn	Can explain why it can be more valuable to work with a partner
Can list three things that can help in problem solving	Can describe how problem solving can be frustrating	Can list the steps in problem solving
Likes to problem solve with diagrams and can give an example	Can describe why a math log would be helpful	Can identify one thing they need to work on in problem solving

C. Secondary Example

FIND SOMEONE WHO . . . ■

Can name three allies in the Second World War	Can explain how the United States entered the Second World War	Can explain why the U.S. was involved in the Vietnam war
Can state some of the technological advances from the Persian Gulf War	Can explain the medical advancements from the First World War	Can share what precipitated the attack on Iraq
Can explain the main issue in the Crimean War	Can predict whether the conflict in Iraq will continue indefinitely	Can discuss similarities of the First and Second World Wars

SELECTED REFERENCES ■

Barell (2003), Bellanca and Forgarty (1994), Hill and Eckert (1995), Hill and Hill (1990), Reid (2002), Robertson and Kagan (1992), Silver, Strong, and Perini (1997)

TEAMING TO LEARN

Four-Corner Cards

◼ PURPOSE AND DESCRIPTION

This strategy could be used as a conversation starter or pre-assessment. It allows students to begin with their knowledge and questions and allows them to share these in a semi-private environment one on one. It gives the teacher the data from which to plan.

Making Connections

Brain Bits	This supports social and active learning and gives students access to new ideas and to integrate the new learning with the old. Also supports cognitive rehearsal, including the development of vocabulary, clarifying, and sharing. This sets up a safe environment for articulation.
Theaters of the Mind	Emotional, Social, Physical, Reflective, and Cognitive Learning
Learning Styles	Beach Ball: creative and random, Puppy: processing, Clipboard: orderly process, Microscope: analytical
Research Basis	Questioning, cues and advanced organizers, non-linguistic representation, using similarities and differences, analogies and metaphors, summarizing and note taking, cooperative learning, generating hypothesis, and cognitive complexity
Grouping	Partners
Grade Level	This technique works for late elementary, middle level, and high school.
Timing	Provide 5 to 10 minutes with prior modeling by teacher. Use prior to a new unit to pre-assess or get baseline data...toward the end of the unit or for a formative assessment during the unit.

STEPS AND DIRECTIONS

1. Give students a card with four sections and four prompts.

2. Each person responds to the prompts in each corner of the card.

3. When students are finished, they can walk about and share their four corners with four other participants.

4. This also sets the stage for planning how to respond to the needs of students.

5. It can also be used for brainstorming purposes as with the life pre-servers shown on page 28.

6. The Life Preserver can be drawn on a large piece of newsprint, and four students can use colored markers to brainstorm in their own section

OTHER NOTES ◼

This can be used for the following conditions:

- Students need some active involvement related to their own wellbeing
- Anytime students need a change of state and another student with whom to discuss an idea
- When students need to move or get up
- The teacher needs to lower the risk for participation
- Dialogue and processing are necessary
- Need for team building

Examples and Uses

PRIMARY (PICTURES AND WORDS) ◼

Related to assessment practices, the card may look like the following:

What do you know about forests?	What would you like to know?
Why do we need forests?	Have you been to a forest? What did you see?

MIDDLE OR HIGH SCHOOL EXAMPLE ◼

This example can be used after introducing the topic, perhaps after a sort video clip or reading a brief article about cell biology and health.

What do you know about cell biology?	What would you like to know about the impacts of cell biology on your health?
Why do we need to know about this aspect of biology?	Have you ever had your blood tested by your doctor? What aspects of cell biology did the doctor and lab use to see if you were healthy?

■ **GRAPHICAL EXAMPLE**

A life preserver is another form of Four Corner. It may be used for brainstorming or pre-assessment.

The life preserver can be divided into as many sections as there are people in the group. It also could be a note taking and summarizing sheet.

Life Preserver

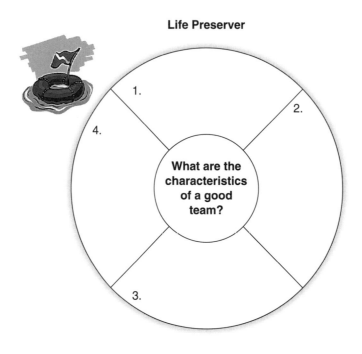

Life Preserver

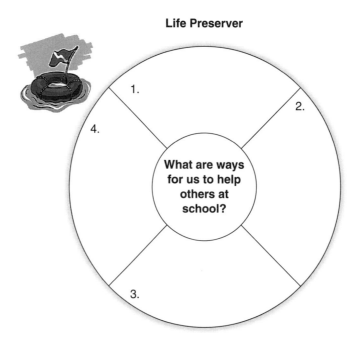

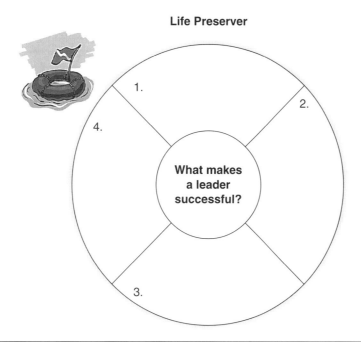

Life Preserver

What makes a leader successful?

1.

2.

3.

4.

SELECTED REFERENCES ■

Gibbs (2001), Hill & Hill (1990), Reid (2002)

TEAMING TO LEARN

Random Partners

■ PURPOSE AND DESCRIPTION

It is important to connect everyone with everyone else. Learners of all ages need dialogue to explore and clarify information so that it can become knowledge. This strategy also forges connections between and among students to create a closer learning community in the classroom.

Making Connections

Brain Bits	This addresses emotional impact and social support and development of cognitive learning in terms of developing common vocabulary; movement suits our need for physical interaction. Humans need to feel connected and included.
Theaters of the Mind	Social, Emotional, Physical, Cognitive, and Reflective Learning
Learning Styles	Microscope, Puppies, Clipboard, Beach Balls
Research Basis	Questioning, cues and advanced organizers, homework review, cooperative group learning
Grouping	Partners
Grade Level	This technique works for late elementary, middle level, and high school.
Timing	Give students an opportunity to connect with all students in the classroom to build community and raise the level of trust and safety.

STEPS AND DIRECTIONS

1. Prepare appointment cards such as small 4x4 cards with a symbol for each season such as a snowman, beach scene, blossoms, and autumn leaves.

2. Students will put their name on their appointment card.

3. Then everyone will walk around and make appointments for each of the seasons.

4. As students meet other students, they will write their partner's name on the appointment card at the season when they plan to meet.

5. They will thank their partner and move on to make another appointment with someone else at a different season time.

6. When they have their four appointments (winter, spring, summer, and fall), they will go back to their table or desk.

7. The teacher can then use the appointment cards to get students together for a discussion or a task at anytime during the day.

8. You can also set up the students in two lines facing each other.

9. The first person across from a student is the first partner, and students will put their name on their card by the first appointment. Then the one line moves one place to the right. The person on the end will come down to the other end and then everyone will have a new partner. That will be their second appointment.

10. The process will continue until all the appointments are filled.

11. Students will need to tape the appointment card into their notebook so that they don't misplace it.

Examples and Uses

1. After a video clip, ask the students to find their _____partner and discuss three things they learned in the video.

2. Meet with your _____ partner and chat about how you solved the problem.

3. Meet with your _____ partner and talk about the homework. What questions do you have?

4. It may be used to read an article or story and discuss the key points.

5. It may be used to complete a graphic organizer together.

6. You may be creative and use appointment cards with special significance to the group, such as seasonal symbols for Halloween, sports events, holidays, and so on.

Find a partner

SPRING _____

WINTER _____

SUMMER

FALL

_____

_____

Clock Partners

1:00 _____

2:00 _____

3:00 _____

4:00 _____

5:00 _____

6:00 _____

7:00 _____

8:00 _____

9:00 _____

10:00 _____

11:00 _____

12:00 _____

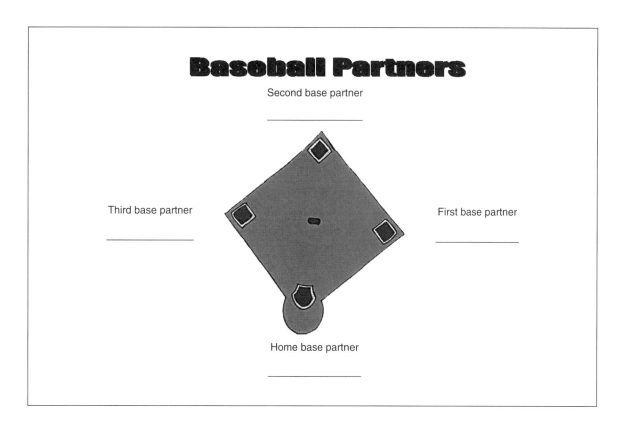

Baseball Partners

Second base partner

_____

Third base partner

_____

First base partner

_____

Home base partner

_____

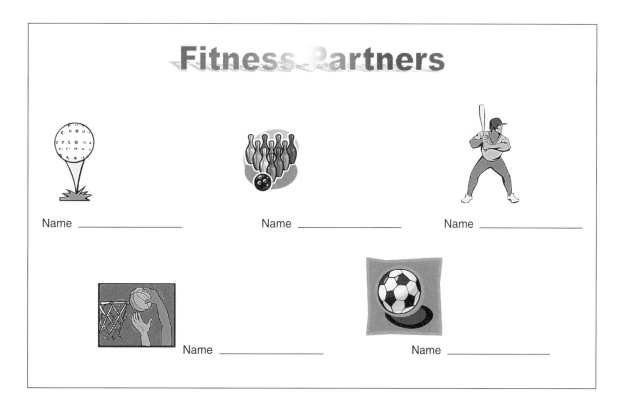

Fitness Partners

Name _____

Name _____

Name _____

Name _____

Name _____

My meetings:

_____

1 _____

2

3 _____

4 _____

5 _____

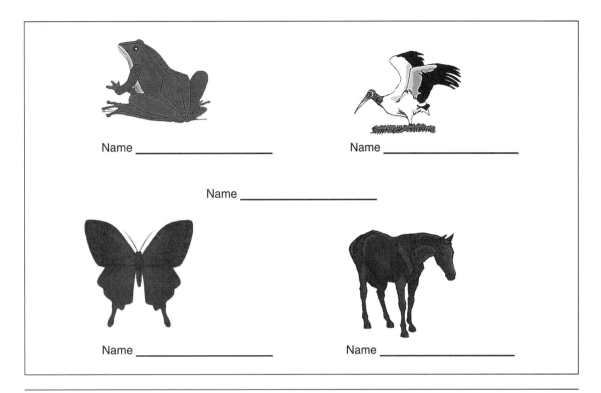

Name _____

Name _____

Name _____

Name _____

Name _____

SELECTED REFERENCES   ■

Adapted from the following: Johnson and Johnson (1989), Kagan (1992a)

TEAMING TO LEARN

T-Chart, Y-Chart

■ PURPOSE AND DESCRIPTION

These charts can be used to compare and contrast as well as for note taking and summarizing. It can be a tool for organizing information and facilitating dialogue. It is also a way to display critical attributes of a concept.

Making Connections

Brain Bits	This process emphasizes the reflective learning system; students think more critically and creatively when given the opportunity to question and analyze a topic deeply. It supports social and active learning and gives students access to new ideas and to integrate the new learning with the old. Also, it supports cognitive rehearsal, including the development of vocabulary, clarifying, and sharing.
Theaters of the Mind	Emotional, Social, Physical, Reflective, and Cognitive Learning
Learning Styles	Beach Ball: creative and random, Puppy: processing, Clipboard: orderly process, Microscope: analytical
Research Basis	Questioning, cues and advanced organizers, non-linguistic representation, using similarities and differences, summarizing and note taking, cooperative learning, generating hypothesis, and cognitive complexity
Grouping	May be done with a partner or in a small group (three).
Grade Level	This technique works for late elementary, middle level, and high school. For younger or less-literate students this could be used as a whole-group discussion tool to model this type of thinking.
Timing	This takes 10 to 20 minutes with prior modeling by teacher. Use with very small groups toward the end of the unit or for a formative assessment during the unit.
Other Notes	These methods also work great as note takers.

■ T-CHART

STEPS AND DIRECTIONS

1. Create a *T* on a sheet of chart paper at each table. For early elementary children, the paper may be folded like a hot dog.

2. Put a title on the page to focus the thinking. One might be "Taking Turns."

3. Label the left side *Looks Like*. Label the right side *Sounds Like*.

4. Ask the students to consider what "Taking Turns" would look like when it works well, and what it sounds like when it works well.

5. After some think-and-discussion time, ask students to contribute ideas that can be written on the common chart.

6. By doing this at each table, it gives students more "air time" and input.

7. Charts can then be posted and perused by participants to look for commonalities.

8. Another large group chart can be created by the whole group after the initial charts are completed and posted.

9. This could become the shared vision of how students work well together.

OTHER NOTES ■

This can be used for the following conditions:

- Students need some active involvement related to their own wellbeing
- Anytime students need a change of state and another colleague to discuss an idea
- When students need to move or get up
- The teacher needs to lower the risk for participation
- Dialogue and creating consensus is necessary
- Need for team building

Examples and Uses

1. Create a clear understanding of a concept. Use *Looks like . . .* and *Sounds like . . . .*

2. Use to define what a concept *is* or *is not*. It might be attentive listening or disagreeing in an agreeable way.

3. A T-chart may be used for concept attainment with yes and no examples.

ARCHAIC

IS	IS NOT

4. It can be used to compare and contrast two concepts such as a *Democracy* and *Communism*.

5. It may be used with headings such as *Cause* and *Effect* related to a topic.

ACTIVE LISTENING

LOOKS LIKE	*SOUNDS LIKE*

COMPARE AND CONTRAST

DEMOCRACY	*COMMUNISM*

COOPERATION

IS	IS NOT

A SUCCESSFUL STUDENT

CAUSE	EFFECT

■ Y-CHART

A Y-chart is a variation of the T-chart. It adds the dimension of emotions to the mix. It pushes students to think about feelings associated with the concept. What would it *Look Like*, *Sound Like*, and *Feel Like*. Tapping into human emotions helps students internalize information and develop empathy for others that will create a safe and growth-oriented climate. It can also be used to organize information for any idea or concept that has three parts. It would work with the jigsaw technique. Each student reads and summarizes part of a topic. You could give students roles so that they rotate roles as they explain and record their part. The roles that might be used could be *Reporter*, *Recorder*, and *Clarifier*. That way everyone is engaged at each step.

Encouraging others

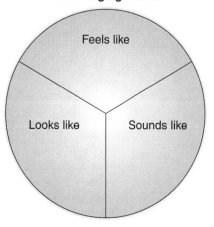

What are good choices for each meal?

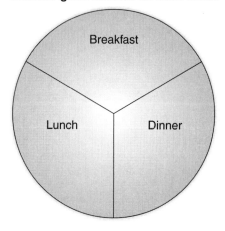

Whose responsibility is it to recycle?

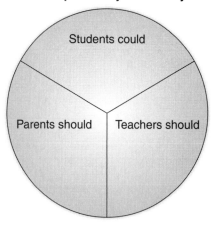

■ SELECTED REFERENCES

Adapted from the following: Hill and Hancock (1993), Johnson, Johnson, and Holubec (1993)

TEAMING TO LEARN

Graffiti

PURPOSE AND DESCRIPTION ■

Graffiti, as we know, is the drawing and writing we see on the sides of buildings and bridges. There is no exact form for this material, just random jottings and paintings. This strategy of Graffiti can be used as a way of brainstorming ideas. It is also a useful process of developing concepts through inductive thinking process. This process includes examining data related to prior knowledge or skill or previously learned material. This quick, low-preparation strategy gives us individual data rather than a collective class impression. It also gives an indication of learning styles (i.e., visual, verbal).

Making Connections

Brain Bits	Students think more critically and creatively when given the opportunity to question and analyze a topic deeply. Graffiti supports social and active learning and gives students access to new ideas and the opportunity to integrate the new learning with the old. Also, it supports cognitive rehearsal, including the development of vocabulary, clarifying, and sharing.
Theaters of the Mind	Emotional, Social, Reflective, Physical, and Cognitive Learning
Learning Styles	Beach Ball: creative and random, Puppy: processing, Clipboard: orderly process, Microscope: analytical
Research Basis	Questioning, cues and advanced organizers, nonlinguistic representation, using similarities and differences, summarizing and note taking, cooperative learning, generating hypothesis, and cognitive complexity
Grouping	Use with groups of three to four students to foster "air time" and opportunities for oral discussion.
Grade Level	This technique works for late elementary, middle level, and high school. For younger or less-literate students this could be used as a whole-group discussion tool to model this type of thinking.
Timing	This takes two or three minutes to introduce the concept and about 90 seconds for brainstorming. Provide two minutes for sharing.
Other Notes	1. This strategy allows all students to be engaged simultaneously. It also opens mental files so that prior knowledge of each student is tapped and assessed. It is also a quick, low-preparation technique. 2. Each student should use a different colored marker so that it highlights his or her ideas.

STEPS AND DIRECTIONS

1. Organize a sheet of chart paper so that each student in the group has a space to use.

2. Suggest a topic so that students have a focus for brainstorming.

3. Allow time for students to think about the topic and collect their thoughts.

4. Have each student jot down the ideas in pictures or words in the space assigned.

5. Have students share their notes in a "round robin" fashion.

6. Students could discuss the topic and come up with a robust question to place in the center box.

■ OTHER NOTES

This can be used with the following conditions:

- Participants need some active involvement related to their own prior knowledge
- Active involvement of personal ideas and kinesthetic task is needed
- Dialogue and sharing are necessary
- Pre-assessment data for planning a unit of study
- Check for understanding during or at the end of the unit

■ PRIMARY GRADE EXAMPLE

1. Three children work in a group together with an organizer as shown in the example on p. 43.

2. Each student would have his or her own space on the page.

3. Each would draw or write symbols and words related to the topic.

4. The prompt might be, "What do you know about the season of winter?"

5. What is a good question about winter that you would like to investigate with your group? Put your question in the box in the center of the page.

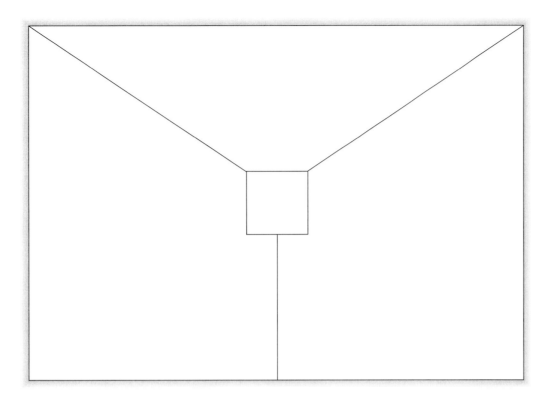

SECONDARY LEVEL EXAMPLE ■

1. Secondary students are examining the following literacy terms: alliteration, pathetic fallacy, onomatopoeia, and analogy.

2. A group of four students will label the four sections of the chart, one with each literacy term.

3. Each student with a marker will brainstorm a definition and example of the term in their section.

4. At the signal, they will rotate the sheet and read and add to the new term in front of them.

5. The page will be rotated until every student has had a chance to contribute to each term.

6. This would make a good review.

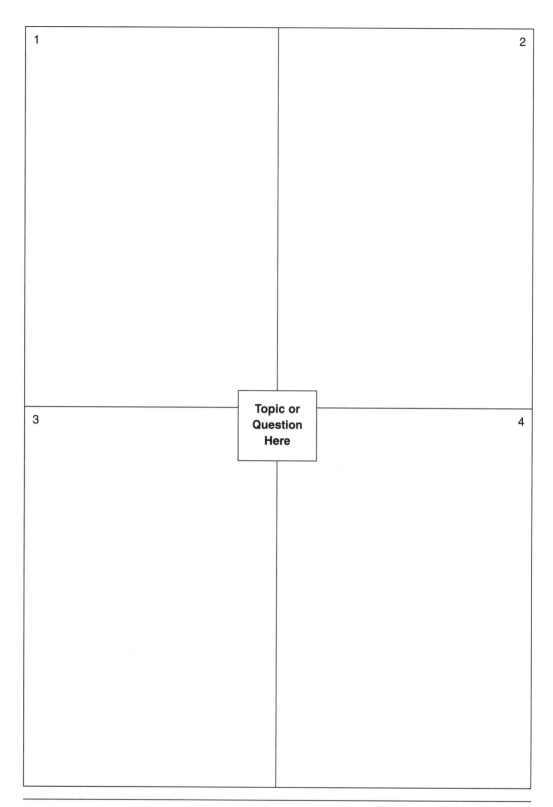

■ SELECTED REFERENCES

Bennett and Rolheiser (2001), Gibbs (2001)

TEAMING TO LEARN
Think-Pair-Share,
Say and Switch

PURPOSE AND DESCRIPTION ■

Think-Pair-Share

Think-Pair-Share is a strategy that increases the time for thinking so that the brain functions using the neocortex, and it makes it safe to voice an opinion or share an understanding in a controlled environment. This strategy facilitates wait time that Mary Budd Rowe (1987) suggests is necessary to receive quality answers from students. The brain takes at least three to five seconds to access information from long-term memory and requires "wait time" to do that. Think-Pair-Share allows time for talk about the topic or concept and increases the quality of thinking and the responses that ensue. Students tend to give "thicker" answers that are well thought out if given time to think, discuss, and elaborate. It is also a great tool to check for understanding. As students are discussing, the teacher is "eavesdropping" and gets a good sense of who knows what or any misconceptions that might be out there.

Say and Switch

Often, when students work with a partner, one person takes over and uses all the air time, not giving the other person a chance to generate and share ideas. This is a strategy to encourage focused discussion, giving equal time to each of the partners and holding each partner accountable. Say and switch is very useful for reviewing, rehearsing, practicing, or checking for understanding. The dialogue helps clarify student thinking; it also develops vocabulary and facilitates long-term memory.

Making Connections

Brain Bits	Seek meaning, relevancy, and connections
Theaters of the Mind	Social, Emotional, Cognitive, Physical, and Reflective Learning
Learning Styles	Microscope, Puppy, Clipboard, Beach Ball, Interpersonal, Analytical, Random
Research Basis	Questioning, cues and advanced organizers, homework, cooperative learning
Grouping	Use student partners.

Grade Level	This technique works for late elementary, middle level, and high school.
Timing	Use toward the end of the unit or for a formative assessment during the unit. Use as a check for understanding. Use as a rehearsal before a quiz or test. Provide five minutes or more.
Other Notes	Use a timer to monitor each partner's turn and keep the process moving along.
	This process fosters active listening.
	Ask questions during group processing to support checking assumptions, author's point of view, and inferential thinking.

STEPS AND DIRECTIONS FOR THINK-PAIR-SHARE

1. A question or idea is presented.
2. The prompt might be, "Think about that to yourself."
3. Give about 30 seconds for students to think.
4. Then say, "Now turn to a partner and share your answer."
5. Pairs discuss for 60 to 90 seconds and then are asked to share with the whole group, another pair, or small group.

■ VARIATIONS ON THINK-PAIR-SHARE

Think-Pair-Draw-Share: Students may use wallpaper posters as part of this process.

Think-Pair-Share-Write or Think-Pair-Write-Share: Students may use any of the graphic-organizer-based strategies and then complete at least one individual piece at the conclusion of a Think-Pair-Share so that the teacher knows which students understand and can apply the learning.

■ OTHER NOTES

This can be used for the following conditions:

- Students need some active involvement related to their own well-being
- Anytime students need a change of state and another person to discuss an idea
- When students need to move or get up
- The teacher needs to lower the risk for participation
- Dialoguing and creating consensus is necessary
- Need for team building
- Formative assessment data is needed quickly (e.g., check for understanding)

EXAMPLES FOR THINK-PAIR-SHARE ■

Primary Reading

Prompt:

What was the reason the farmer decided to sell the cow?

What else could he have done?

What are the parts to a plant?

Draw it and label the parts with your partner.

Middle School

Prompt:

What are the reasons that students bully other students?

Discuss reasons with your partner.

Be ready to share your ideas.

or

Think about how the seasons change from spring to summer, summer to fall, and fall to winter.

Share with your partner why the seasons change.

Decide on a way to share this with the group.

High School

Prompt:

What do you think is the most important issue that the new president should tackle?

Why is it the highest priority in your opinion?

Think to yourself.

or

Considering what happened in the chapter you read last night, what would you predict will happen next and why?

Discuss with your partner and be ready to answer.

STEPS AND DIRECTIONS ■
FOR SAY AND SWITCH

1. Have students get a partner and letter off *A* and *B*.

2. Share the topic or prompt.

3. Give students a moment to think about what they might say.

4. Starting with Student A, give the student 60 seconds to begin the conversation.

5. Call, "switch."

6. Student B will pick up the thread of the dialogue and add more information for another 60 seconds.

7. Repeat another round or two.

8. Open up the large group discussion after students have had the opportunity to generate and develop ideas.

9. You can end with an individual reflection to pull all that great thinking together.

■ EXAMPLE FOR PRIMARY GRADES SAY AND SWITCH

Prompt:
Explain what the weather is like in the winter in the north.

- Talk about the sports people play.
- Describe the clothes people wear in winter.
- Add special events or holidays unique to that region.
- What is a favorite thing you would enjoy in the winter if you lived here?
- You and your partner can use a graffiti sheet to jot down words or pictures.

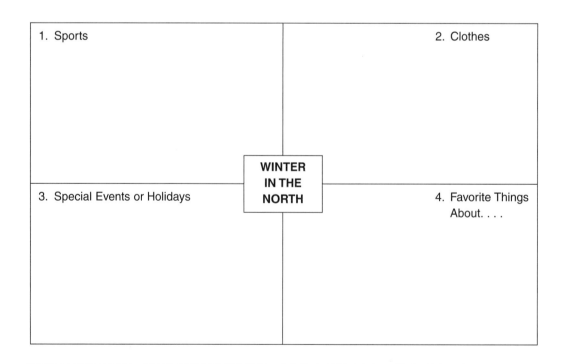

EXAMPLE FOR MIDDLE ■ GRADES SAY AND SWITCH

Prompt:

You have read the next scene in *Romeo and Juliet*. With your partner, start to tell the sequence of events in this chapter.

- Use a timeline or storyboard format to chronicle the order of events. In addition, a sequence map or a series of sticky notes would work with this prompt.
- End with a partner or individual prompt to pull thinking together such as, "Which event in the sequence was most critical to the outcome of the story?"

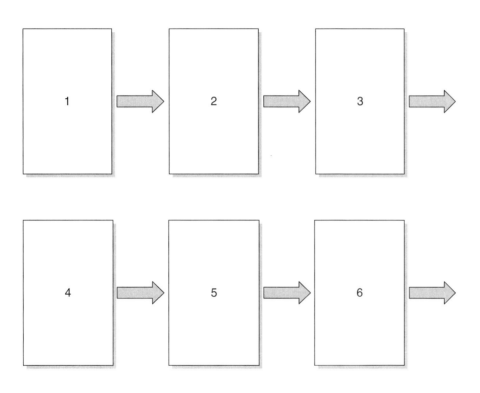

Which event in the sequence was most critical to the outcome of the story?

■ EXAMPLES FOR SECONDARY GRADES SAY AND SWITCH

Prompt:
Discuss the pros and cons of a government bailout of the automotive industry.

- Use this graphic organizer or one like it.
- As a final activity and an individual accountability piece, have students take a personal point of view and justify it.

Pros of Government Bailout	Cons of Government Bailout

My point of view? Why?

SECONDARY EXAMPLE SAY AND SWITCH OR THINK-PAIR-SHARE   ■

Prompt:

Review notes from our current unit. Discuss this with a partner using the Processing Pause Graphic Organizer.

- Use the confusing pieces as points to start a review prior to a test.
- Use a check for key understanding about the unit before proceeding with new learning.

Processing Pause

The Most Important Facts and Vocabulary in This Unit	Pictures and Graphics That Help You Understand This Unit
Questions or Points of Confusion	
Summary of Key Ideas From Your Discussion	

SELECTED REFERENCES   ■

Hartzler and Henry (1994), Hoffman and Olson-Ness (1996), Kagan, (1992a), Kuzmich (2003), Lyman and McTighe (2001), Marzano, Norford, Paynter, Gaddy, and Pickering (2004)

3

Sharing Knowledge and Skills

Introduction

Student teams that learn by sharing knowledge and skills achieve more and do so with greater effectiveness than students who learn the same material individually (Johnson & Johnson, 1997). Besides higher achievement and greater retention, cooperation, compared with competitive or individualistic efforts, tends to result in more benefits (Johnson & Johnson, 1989):

Added Benefits of Teamwork That Increase Learning Performance	Why is this important for turning knowledge into skill development? Why and how do these teaming benefits work?
Willingness to persist despite difficulty of the learning	Cognitive dissonance is uncomfortable feelings caused by new learning when we don't yet feel capable or fully understand. It takes persistence to work through this normal period of uncertainty about our knowledge and skill level.
Long-term retention of what is learned	Newly learned material is difficult to retain without concrete experiences, visualization, and the making of personal meaning. Groups' interaction facilitates all three.
Higher level critical thinking	It is essential to knowledge and skill acquisition that we use the frontal lobes of the brain where higher level cognition is processed. Justifying responses and coming to agreement in teams support the whole brain as we learn new things and further develop already learned knowledge into skill.
Creativity of thinking	Applying knowledge to skill development and adapting what you know to new situations takes creativity. A team provides a venue for rapid rehearsal, blending and building off each other's ideas, and hypotheses testing when groups develop skills together.
Positive attitude	The brain cannot really retain or use knowledge without a positive attitude about what is learned *or* the people we are learning with. Either works, but we must have at least one to develop memory of learning.
Transfer of learning from one situation to another	Developing skill from knowledge requires use to transfer what we know from known to unknown situations for long-term retention and adaptation of learning. Transfer is expedited when we see situations played out through a teaming process.
Time on task	Our brains require us to be alert and attentive when we learn, or no memory or skill acquisition will occur. Individuals tune in and out of learning more frequently than students who have to stay alert as part of team interaction.

SOURCE: Seven benefits portion of this table adapted from http://www.co-operation.org/pages/SIT.html

Learning content knowledge, or any knowledge for that matter, requires us to take in the information through our senses, determine our emotional response (safe, unsafe, etc.), and then to create associations with prior learning before we can retain the new knowledge or use it at higher levels of thinking. These associations require us to have some background experiences to connect the new learning to and access the critical neural pathways for retaining additional connections and knowledge. In a differentiated classroom, if students come to us without much background knowledge, we need to give them opportunities to make new connections through information, media, and through other learners. When we do that, we create metaphors, similes that connect the new learning, or we can create these connections based on social interaction as well. Teaming has been shown to be very powerful when used to make these critical connections prior to developing the skill and application of learning. The strategies in this section of the book seek to support that element of connection building through flexible grouping in a formal and organized fashion or sometimes randomly, since that has the greatest payoff for transfer, thinking, on task behaviors, creativity, retention of learning, and a willingness to persist even when the learning is difficult. This is a positive formula to maximize the research-based impact of teaming and formal yet active tools for learning.

All of the strategies in this chapter have the added advantage of easy differentiation. Each can be used to extend flexible grouping by interest area or need; each can support great open-ended questions, prompts, and activities. The processes meet diverse learner needs in terms of challenge with support and a clear connection to rigorous learning. Students support each other in these groupings using great graphic organizers and content-appropriate conversations. Teachers can also vary the materials and resources students use to contribute to these strategies to add a customized piece of differentiation for students who function at various levels of literacy or skill in the content.

Some groups work better than others to expand learning options and increase skill development from the deep understanding of knowledge. Not all groups are cooperative groups (Johnson & Johnson, 1997). Placing students into groups by seating them together and telling students they are to cooperate to do their work does not cause the kind of effect size results we want to see. Groups may be classified into at least four categories (Johnson & Johnson, 1997):

1. *Pseudo groups* are groups whose members have been assigned to work together, but they have no interest in doing so and are very competitive. Where roles are not used or rehearsed, students may block each other's achievement, communicate poorly, confuse each other, loaf, and seek a free ride. The result is that this type of group does not assist itself or the individuals who make it.

2. *Traditional groups* are groups whose members agree to work together but see little benefit from doing so. There is individualistic work with some talking but not real sharing or discourse. Members interact primarily to share information and clarify how to complete the tasks. Then they each do the work on their own. Their achievements are individually recognized and rewarded. The result is that some individuals may benefit and some not.

3. "*Cooperative groups* are groups whose members commit themselves to the common purposes of maximizing their own and each other's success. Their defining characteristics are a compelling purpose to maximize all members' productivity and achievement, holding themselves and each other accountable for contributing their share of the work to achieve the group's goals, promoting each other's success by sharing resources, and providing each other support and encouragement, using social skills to coordinate their efforts and achieve their goals, and analyzing how effectively they are achieving their goals and working together. The result is that the sum of the whole is greater than the potential of the individual members." (Adapted from http://www.co-operation.org/pages/SIT.html)

4. *High-performance cooperative groups* are groups that meet all the criteria for a cooperative group and outperform all expectations, given their particular membership or desire of the members.

The conditions for success described in the third type of group articulated by Johnson and Johnson (1997) on their Web site are possible to achieve. This is a list of the conditions that must be taught and rehearsed for successful grouping that results in higher level thinking, great problem solving, and productive collaboration.

Eight Teaming Building Blocks to Teach and Rehearse in Order to Maximize the Effectiveness of Student Teams

8. Analyzing how effectively the team worked together

7. Establishing rituals for feedback and celebration

6. Establishing a means of gathering and sharing resources

5. Setting group and individual goals for contributing to the teaming process and success

4. Developing the ability to picture successful teaming and each student's contribution to that success

3. Developing common understanding of learning tasks and criteria for learning success

2. Developing respectful social skills and good communication to coordinate efforts

1. Building a knowledge of each other, each other's styles, and an appreciation of the diversity that makes teams better performing

We used these criteria as we selected and developed the strategies in this section of the book. We feel strongly that well-rehearsed process and communication are worth the time teaching and practicing, and these should be reviewed with each grouping opportunity. By paying close attention to the criteria for successful cooperative groups, we can achieve more sharing of knowledge and developing of skills to apply that knowledge so that students do the following:

- Demonstrate the learning of content
- Develop understanding about that content
- Develop learning strategies applicable to the content
- Learn multiple routines to turn knowledge into skill
- Transfer new knowledge and skills to more complex tasks
- Expand options for future learning
- Share and celebrate successes
- Provide each other with needed peer support

We hope you find these teaming strategies effectively build student knowledge and application of that knowledge to build transferable and adaptive skills for current and future learning.

SHARING KNOWLEDGE AND SKILLS
ABC Conversations

PURPOSE AND DESCRIPTION ■

This strategy gives students a chance to listen intently to one person at a time and offers a captive audience. It allows for a sharing of ideas or problem solving.

It makes a good processing tool at the end of a session so that individual students can share their analysis, applications, and questions about an idea or topic. It can also be used to start off learning using text or other resources to share new information that includes more critical thinking than a lecture or "lecturette." The trio could be designed with the same level of student readiness or students in a heterogeneous trio so that "cross-pollination" of good ideas can be sparked. In a differentiated classroom, teachers may use ABC conversations to collect informal formative assessment so that the next learning activities may be differentiated.

Making Connections

Brain Bits	This process emphasizes the impact of deeper thinking using collaborative learning and developing patterns and connections. Learning to restate information in your own words and formulate questions are key learning strategies that use more of the brain for processing and thereby increase memory and connections.
Theaters of the Mind	Reflective, Social, Physical, and Cognitive Learning
Learning Styles	Beach Ball: creativity, Microscope: problem solving, Clipboard: process-based thinking, Puppy: processing, Interpersonal: sequential
Research Basis	Questioning, cues and advanced organizers, analysis, scaffolding thinking, metacognition strategies, generating questions
Grouping	Use with groups of three students, each with specific roles that can be rotated.
Grade Level	This technique works for late elementary, middle level, and high school. For younger or less-literate students, this could be used as a role-play with the rest of the students looking on; with rehearsal, even young students can use ABC Conversations effectively. Younger students may need picture promotes or books to use as stimulus for the conversation.
Timing	• Provide 10 to 30 minutes depending on the prompts and roles. Be certain to model use of the templates and the roles in the conversation technique. • Use at the beginning of the unit for new learning, in the middle of the unit to deepen understanding, or at the end of the unit for review.

(Continued)

(Continued)

Other Notes	• Prepare and walk through a model with students first. • English language learners and some types of learning disabled students may need leveled written material if you are using this technique for new learning or for processing information. • Assign roles in the triad and make certain each student can perform each role as you rotate. • See 3–2–1 as this could be used easily with ABC conversations. • This works well on discrete bits of learning and information and short pieces of text, single chart, map, or graph and could be used as an electronic dialogue sharing a chat site. • Prepare the scribe form and add prompts as needed. • Diverse students may need a list of questions to ask to help deepen understanding.

STEPS AND DIRECTIONS

1. Form triads.

2. Each person takes a letter: *A, B, C.*

3. Person A is the Questioner.

   Person B is the Respondent.

   Person C is the Scribe.

4. In the first round, each performs his or her role.

5. In the second round, each performs a new role (see chart at top of p. 59).

6. In the third round, each performs a new role.

Notes: ABC Conversations can be used in at least two ways

1. ABC Read and Converse: Use this as a buddy reading-and-thinking method by having the roles include reading and putting the information in your own words and then have the group do the scribe form. This is a great differentiation method with a diverse class. You can use level materials or ask peers to help each other with the text, document, or other source.

2. ABC Conversation: Use this as a discussion tool to deepen understanding of new learning, add to skill or application of knowledge, or review learning prior to an assessment. Students converse with or without notes to offer their understanding and further reflections or questions.

■ SELECTED REFERENCES

Buehl (2006), Chadwick (2006), Elder and Paul (2002), Gregory and Kuzmich (2007), Lipton, Humbard, and Wellman (2001)

Round One	Round Two	Round Three
A Questioner	B Questioner	C Questioner
B Respondent	C Respondent	A Respondent
C Scribe	A Scribe	B Scribe

Scribe Form Example A

	Notes:	Reflections:
Person A _____		
Person B _____		
Person C _____		

Scribe Form Example B

	Notes:	Questions:
Person A _____		
Person B _____		
Person C _____		

SOURCE: Gregory and Kuzmich (2007).

■ SECONDARY EXAMPLE FOR ABC READ AND CONVERSE FOR NEW LEARNING

Scribe Form for Reasons for Building "Green"

Use provided article; read and review together.

ABC Read

1. First Person reads a sentence or two and puts it in his or her own words; others may comment or add information.

2. Second Person reads the next sentence or section and puts it in his or her own words; others may comment or add information.

3. Third Person reads the next sentence or section and puts it in his or her own words; others may comment or add information.

4. Repeat until the article is completely read and reviewed.

5. Use this template to gather summary notes and formulate questions for further investigation or study.

	Notes:	Questions:
Person A: Tom	Green building helps reduce each person's carbon footprint.	Why doesn't every home builder use this approach since we know so much about carbon exchange and reduction?
Person B: Rita	Green building uses renewable resources.	What other renewable resources can be used in both home and commercial building?
Person C: Carlos	Green building uses products that reduce pollution involving the creation of the products and makes the green building less polluting as well.	Some materials that are sold as "green" actually cause more of a carbon footprint similar to the current problem with biofuel used in vehicles. Why don't producers of these "green" products and builders seek to solve these problems? Why is this "false" advertising about being green allowed? Are there any government regulations for what is considered "green"?

■ ABC CONVERSATION ABOUT ALREADY LEARNED MATERIAL

Scribe Form for World War II and the Holocaust

Process

Follow the rules above for ABC Conversation taking turns as scribe, questioner, and respondent.

	Notes:	Reflections:
Person A: Louis	The people of Denmark did a great deal to save the Jews and others from concentration camps.	I am concerned that more people did not do what these brave people did. I wonder if they feared so much for their lives that they could not find the courage.
Person B: Stephanie	There is speculation that Hitler and some of his leaders were mentally ill in order to commit such horrendous crimes.	I wonder why more people in Germany did not see their actions as "sick" and do something about it. Was this the times; were they brainwashed or just afraid?
Person C: William	Reading the documents from this time period was quite revealing. The precision of the schedules and data kept, the records and diaries give us a real glimpse into a German society consumed with fear and power.	The trials at Nuremberg used so many of these documents. I wonder why people did not destroy this incriminating evidence. These documents made the history and horror come alive for me and made the people so real. They could have been my neighbors.

Examples for Elementary

ABC CONVERSATIONS ABOUT FAIRY TALES ■

Process

1. Follow the rules for ABC Conversations.

2. In the notes, add one thing you know about all fairy tales.

3. In the questions, ask one what if question that might have changed the any of the fairy tales we read.

Scribe Form for Fairy Tales

	Notes:	Questions:
Person A: Thomas	Fairy tales all have a happy ending.	What if the hero never meets the person who has to be rescued?
Person B: Jenny	Fairy tales have a hero and someone that needs help.	What if the hero needs help with some of the things he or she has to do?
Person C: Louisa	Fairy tales have actions that the hero must take to win a prize or a bride.	What if the prize was stolen when the hero gets done?

This could easily lead to writing or telling the students' own fairy tales with unusual twists and building greater creativity and critical thinking about this genre.

■ ELEMENTARY EXAMPLE FOR ABC READ AND CONVERSE FOR NEW LEARNING

Scribe Form for Reasons for Plant Life Cycles Selection

Use provided article; read and review together.

ABC Read

1. First Person reads a sentence or two and puts it in his or her own words; others may comment or add information.

2. Second Person reads the next sentence or section and puts it in his or her own words; others may comment or add information.

3. Third Person reads the next sentence or section and puts it in his or her own words; others may comment or add information.

4. Repeat until the article is completely read and reviewed.

5. Use this template to gather summary notes and formulate questions for further investigation or study.

	Notes:	Questions:
Person A: Anthony	Plants start as seeds.	Where do seeds come from?
Person B: Riga	Plants have flowers, leaves, fruit, or other things they produce.	What makes some plants die in the winter and others stay alive?
Person C: Kim	Plants need water and sunlight and soil to grow.	Why do some plants in my yard grow OK in the shade?

SHARING KNOWLEDGE AND SKILLS
3-2-1 Processing

PURPOSE AND DESCRIPTION ■

This strategy helps students solidify their learning by sorting through relevant and irrelevant information, summarizing, and connecting learning. With the right prompts, this strategy is a great prewriting tool, goal-setting template, or can even get students to see relevant application of newer learning. Depending on the grouping and peer work that teachers use along with this strategy, 3–2–1 can also be an excellent basis for differentiation. Used with Inside-Outside Circle (Kagan, 1992a & 1992b), Consulting Line, or partners and triads, students can consult peers and add to or refine their 3–2–1 card, foldable, or chart.

Making Connections

Brain Bits	Emotional impact and social support, development of cognitive learning in terms of developing common vocabulary, clarifying, and sharing
Theaters of the Mind	Social, Cognitive, and Reflective Learning are part of this strategy. In addition, if you add movement to join a partner in another part of the room, share using Inside-Outside Circle, or act out your 3–2–1, it can be Physical.
Learning Styles	Puppy: processing, Clipboard: organized, Microscope: detail, Interpersonal: sequential
Research Basis	Summarizing, classifying, practice, cues, advanced organizers, and question use or formulation
Grouping	Individual at the closing of class or small groups of two to four; could also be used for sharing with a whole group strategy like Inside-Outside Circle.
Grade Level	Second through twelfth with modification for level of prompt; could be pictorial for primary or a shared writing activity.
Timing	Provide 5 minutes with older students to write and then share; could take from 5 to 20 minutes depending on the prompt.
	Sharing could take place first, providing access to varied information for diverse students and then write after gathering information from peers.
	You could also have students create a brief summary or analysis paragraph upon completion of sharing and 3–2–1; this would take 5 (secondary) to 30 (elementary) minutes depending on age of students.
Other Notes	If students are struggling with the new learning, try sharing prior to completing 3–2–1.
	Use Inside-Outside Circle as a differentiation strategy; students could start a 3–2–1 and then add to it after consulting with peers.
	Provide 3–2–1 cards or charts for students to fill out or make a 3–2–1 foldable with a piece of paper divided into three sections.
	You could also have students develop their own 3–2–1 prompts and respond to them or have them develop a 3–2–1 for another student or a group of peers to respond to.

STEPS AND DIRECTIONS

Basic Process

1. Give students one 3–2–1 card to fill out and then share with a partner.

2. Turn card in as an informal assessment or assignment.

3. Use for both closings and openings to check for understanding, reach application- or analysis-level responses, or practice summarizing.

Prewriting Process

1. Give students a 3–2–1 card to fill out and share with a small group.

2. Ask students to turn the 3–2–1 card into a short summary or analysis paragraph—could put 3–2–1 at top of page and paragraph at bottom.

3. Turn in card and paragraph as an informal assessment of new learning connections and understanding or as demonstration of application depending on the prompt.

Differentiation Process

1. Give partners or triads an opportunity to rehearse their thinking about 3–2–1 out loud. This may be all you do with early primary. For older students, follow the next few steps.

2. Now write your 3–2–1 card or write with a partner.

3. Turn in as above.

Other Options

1. Complete Step 2 or Step 1 and 2 above.

2. Form the class into Inside-Outside Circles or a Consulting Line.

3. Students share 3–2–1.

4. Students add to or refine their 3–2–1 based on the input of peers.

Note: You can also have students do Inside-Outside Circle or Consulting Line prior to even completing the 3–2–1 card. You can add a final summary, analysis, and/or application paragraph if you wish additional information about student thinking and new learning understanding.

■   SELECTED REFERENCES

Adapted from Gregory and Kuzmich (2005a, 2005b), Gregory and Kuzmich (2007), Garmston (1996), Jones (1998), Zygouris-Coe, Wiggins, and Smith (2004)

3-2-1 Processing Examples

3–2–1 TEMPLATE: ADD PROMPTS ■

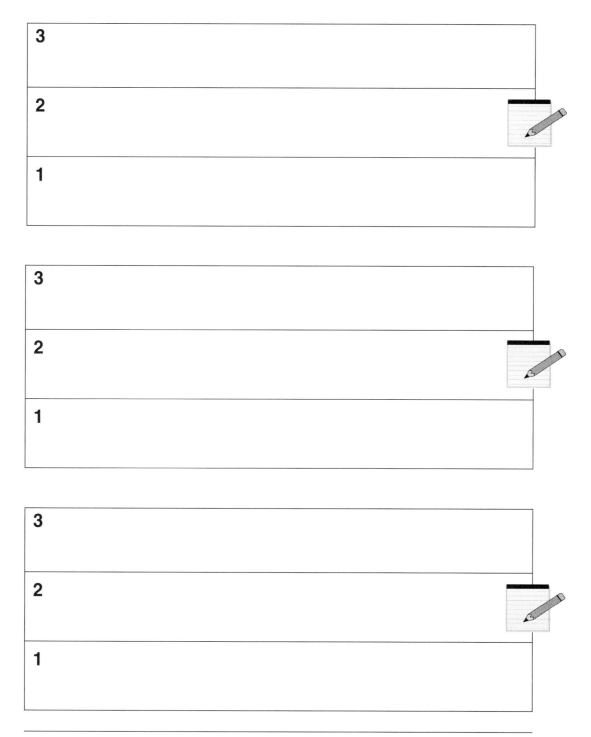

3-2-1 "What's On Your Mind?" Template

"What's On Your Mind?" is another reflective technique that can be used to end a class. It gives students a chance to reflect and share their thinking with others and is a great check for understanding. Use this modification with students fourth grade and up. Vary the prompts as needed and as they apply to learning for the day or for the unit of study so far. Prompts can also get information about students' feelings and interests. Then the teacher has quick, simple formative data that will lead to more precise planning and grouping for the next day or lesson in order to differentiate instruction.

■ WHAT'S ON YOUR MIND?

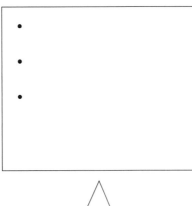

3 ideas that I remember from class

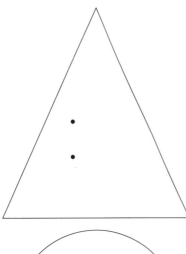

2 ways this learning impacts my life

1 question I have about our learning today

3-2-1 Processing

SECONDARY EXAMPLES ■

3	Things that interest me about . . . .
2	Ways I could use . . . .
1	Things I wonder about . . . .

3	Ways this is used in the real world
2	Things this is similar to
1	Question that this brings to mind

3	Ways this is controversial
2	Two ways people resist . . . .
1	Way people support . . . .

■ **WHAT'S ON YOUR MIND?**

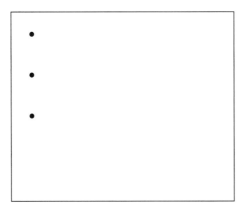

3 ideas that squared with my values and belief

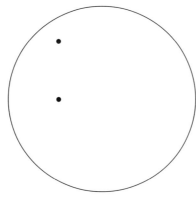

2 ideas rolling around in my head

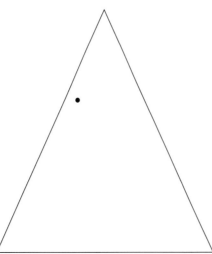

1 idea that piqued my curiosity

ELEMENTARY EXAMPLES ■

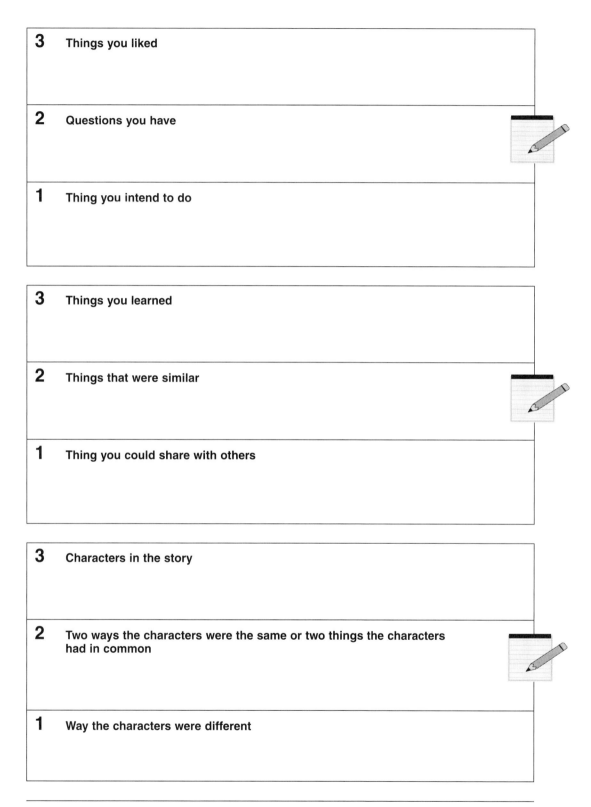

3   Things you liked

2   Questions you have

1   Thing you intend to do

3   Things you learned

2   Things that were similar

1   Thing you could share with others

3   Characters in the story

2   Two ways the characters were the same or two things the characters had in common

1   Way the characters were different

Group Processing Strategies: Consulting Line and Inside-Outside Circle

Many of the templates and organizers in this book can be used with these grouping strategies. Both of these strategies provide opportunities for verbal rehearsal in a safe, supportive way. They are really "one-on-one" conversations that appeal to the auditory, kinesthetic learners in the classroom. They help students clarify their thinking, check for understanding, and use vocabulary of the discipline.

■ CONSULTING LINE

Process Directions

1. Set up the room with two rows of chairs facing each other, close enough to carry on a conversation.

2. One row will be labeled *Consultants* and the other *Clients*.

3. The Clients As will state a problem or issues and the Consultants Bs opposite them will make some practical suggestions that may be helpful for the situation. Allow about two to three minutes for this first step.

4. After the time allowed, the Clients move one chair to their right, and the last person in the row will move to the other end.

5. The Client asks the same question to a new Consultant and records the suggestion given in two to three minutes of time.

6. Then the rows switch roles. The Clients As become Consultants and Consultants Bs become Clients.

7. The process is then repeated with the new Clients asking a question or presenting a problem to the new Consultants, and they go from there.

8. Two rounds may be used.

9. Then each individual reflects on the suggestions he or she has been given and decides to implement or try one or two of the most promising ideas that have been offered.

■ SELECTED REFERENCES

Chadwick (2006), Australian Government DOE (2006), Gregory and Kuzmich (2007), Gibbs (2001)

Round 1 and 2

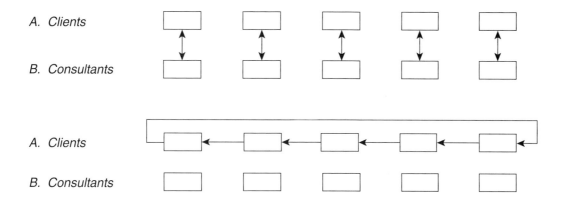

A. Clients

B. Consultants

A. Clients

B. Consultants

Round 3 and 4

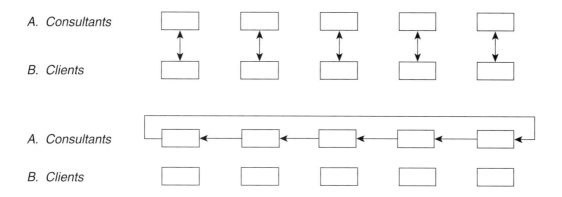

A. Consultants

B. Clients

A. Consultants

B. Clients

■ **INSIDE-OUTSIDE CIRCLE**

Process Directions

1. Put several people—more than three—in a circle facing outward.

2. Put an equal number of people in an outer circle, each one facing one person in the inner circle.

3. Give participants a prompt that encourages reflection or application of thinking.

4. Inside person speaks first.

5. Outside person responds.

6. Each Outside Circle person moves two places (people) clockwise.

7. Repeat Steps 4, 5, and 6 one or two more times, depending on size of circles.

8. You can also change the order of who talks or responds first.

■ **SELECTED REFERENCES**

Australian Government DOE (2006), Chadwick (2006), Johnson, Johnson, & Holubec (1993), Kagan (1992a, 1992b), Gibbs (2001), Gregory and Kuzmich (2007)

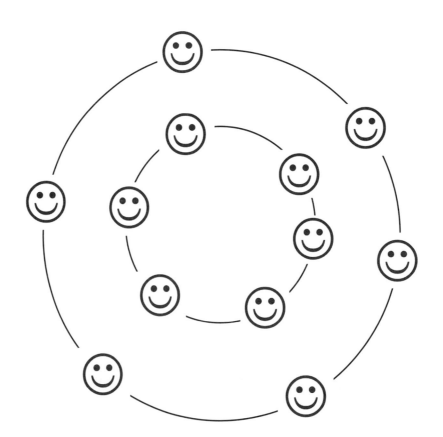

SHARING KNOWLEDGE AND SKILLS
Jigsaw Methods

PURPOSE AND DESCRIPTION ■

There are three types of jigsaw that can be used to process information, deepen comprehension, and facilitate dialogue. Jigsaw uses peer teaching and sharing to further understanding and gives students an active role in learning large amounts of material in an interactive manner that increases long-term memory and supports the use of connections and social learning.

Simple Jigsaw: You may use a simple square jigsaw of three or four students. Each student must become knowledgeable about one piece of information in a table group and then teach the new information to the rest of the group.

Expert Jigsaw: This is similar to the Simple Jigsaw, except each expert from all the groups will join together with the other experts to discuss the material before teaching it back to the original group.

Table Jigsaw: Each table is responsible for a different piece of content. Each table studies the material and decides how to teach it to the large group.

Making Connections

Brain Bits	This process emphasizes the impact of group sharing and dialoguing to learn, comprehend, and make connections. Learning to restate newly learned information in your own words is a key learning and memory strategy.
Theaters of the Mind	Reflective, Social, Physical, and Cognitive Learning
Learning Styles	Beach Ball: creativity, Microscope: problem solving, Clipboard: process-based thinking, Puppy: processing, Interpersonal: sequential and random
Research Basis	Questioning, cues and advanced organizers, analysis, application, evaluation and synthesis, cooperative grouping, examples and nonexamples, verbal rehearsal of new learning, stating things in your own words, teaching others
Grouping	See notes on three types of jigsaw for specific grouping directions.
Grade Level	This technique works well for late elementary, middle level, and high school. For younger or less-literate students, start with a simple jigsaw on known topics to practice the technique, using expert group for older students.
Timing	Provide 10 to 45 minutes depending on the prompts and roles. Be certain to model use of the questions and the roles in the conversation for learning, use of the templates, as well as requiring students to orally report. Use at the beginning of the unit for new learning or to build further understanding as the unit progresses. Using notes and examples from a unit can also be a great review technique prior to assessment.
Other Notes	Prepare and walk through a model with students first. English language learners and some students with learning disabilities may need leveled written material if you are using this technique for new learning or for processing information.

STEPS AND DIRECTIONS

Simple Square

1. Each group is formed with several members. Each person letters off *A*, *B*, *C*, or *D*. Each person in the group has a particular part to become expert with and to share with the group of four.

Expert Jigsaw

Note: This is especially important if students are reading new or complex materials. In the expert groups, the teacher can monitor the clarity and summarizing of information or skills and prevent students from "ruminating ignorance" when they share with their base group. In a differentiated classroom with a variety of reading levels and prior knowledge, expert jigsaw is valuable as students access information, discuss, and explain so that they are clarifying and deepening their knowledge.

1. Each group is formed with several members. Each student letters off *A*, *B*, *C*, or *D*. This is the base group.

2. After each student has a letter, a part of the reading, article, chapter, or part of the overall task is assigned to each student.

3. Then all the As, Bs, Cs, and Ds meet as four new groups to read, discuss, or complete their part of the task. Direct students to four corners of the room (A, B, C, D) to do their "expert" task.

4. When the task is complete or material is learned, the experts return to their base group to share their part of the jigsaw.

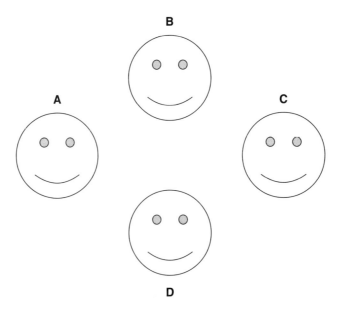

Table Jigsaw

1. Instead of each student in the group lettering off and going off to an expert group, the entire group becomes an expert and presents its part to the other groups.

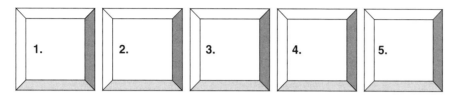

Templates, Examples, and Uses

- **Simple Jigsaw:** Sometimes reading and information gathering can be difficult for students. Using a jigsaw can be a way of facilitating reading comprehension and dialoguing about important aspects of curriculum content. Using a simple square can be a way of initiating that discussion through acquiring, discussing, and contemplating ideas and information and turning them into knowledge through dialogue. Each student will read, find, or watch for a part of the article and/or information or video and then share their information with the table group.

Use this template for any age, even pictorial reporting from younger students. This can be used as a note taker for individual students or as a group note taker for later use.

Information from Student A	Information from Student B
Information from Student C	Information from Student D

or

Use this template for secondary or to differentiate work for late elementary and above.

What is this about? Student A	What are some examples? Student B
What are some uses; what is the function or purpose? Student C	What connections can you make to other learning or experiences? Student C

- Expert Jigsaw:

  Step 1. When students are reading a book or other sources for information, you may have four people in each group. They would letter off *A, B, C, D*. This is the base or home group. People divide up a chapter in equal or appropriate sections for the four or five people in the group. These groups should be heterogeneous based on readiness, reading levels, learning styles, and so on—thus supporting differentiated instruction.

  Step 2. All the As, would meet together, read their parts, and summarize key points. Then decide on the best way to share or teach their base group what they have become expert in. Similarly, Bs, Cs, Ds would do the same with their content or section.

  Step 3. The base or home group would reconvene, and each person in turn would share their part with the other members. An advanced organizer could be used so each person can capture the key points of each section.

Main Topic	
Subheading:	*Notes:*
A.	
B.	
C.	
D.	
E.	

- **Table Jigsaw:** This strategy can also be used to view a video with each table group looking for specific information as to one aspect of the concept being explored. For example, while watching a video about content with multiple concepts taught, each table group uses an advanced organizer to collect information about the following:

WHY? WHAT? HOW? WHEN? ■

Why?	What?
How?	**When?**

SELECTED REFERENCES ■

Aronson, Blaney, Stephin, Sikes, and Snapp (1978), Bennett, Rolheiser, and Stevahn (1991), Gregory and Kuzmich (2007), Hertz-Lazarowitz, Kagan, Sharan, Slavin, and Webb (1985), Hill and Hill (1990), Johnson, Johnson, and Holubec (1993), Slavin (1994)

SHARING KNOWLEDGE AND SKILLS
Concept Formation

■ PURPOSE AND DESCRIPTION

This is an inductive thinking strategy developed by Hilda Taba (1967). It facilitates classification and higher-order thinking. Students receive or generate a data set and discuss, categorize, and label groupings based on like attributes. It is much more student centered and uses a less teacher-directed approach.

Making Connections

Brain Bits	This supports social and active learning and gives students access to new ideas and the ability to integrate the new learning with the old. Also supports cognitive rehearsal, including the development of vocabulary, clarifying, categorizing, pattern recognition, and sharing.
Theaters of the Mind	Social, Cognitive, and Reflective Learning
Learning Styles	Beach Ball: creative and random; Puppy: processing; Clipboard: orderly process; Microscope: analytical
Research-Based	Questioning, cues and advanced organizers, non-linguistic representation, categorization and organization of vocabulary connections, using similarities and differences, cooperative learning, and cognitive complexity
Grouping	This strategy works well with groups of four to six. It can be used with groups of two or three for older students who have more background knowledge or literacy skills and more complex prompts.
Grade Level	This works well for second to twelfth grade. For Pre-K through first students can generate picture cards to sort and categories or use cards already developed.
Timing	This whole sequence can take 15 to 45 minutes depending on the complexity of the prompt, size of the group and the amount of additional processing opportunities created by the teacher, such as writing a summary at the end of the activity.
Other Notes	Make certain to have plenty of sticky notes available. It also helps to have color pens or markers for the category title.
	Students may need some rehearsal to get the category titles at the lower grades.
	English Language Learners and Special Education students may benefit from an article or piece of text at their level or their personal notes from previous instruction so they can draw vocabulary words from text rather than just background knowledge or recall of previous lessons.

STEPS AND DIRECTIONS

1. Suggest a topic so that participants have a focus for brainstorming a data set.

2. Give each student in the group at least five to six sticky notes.

3. Have each student jot down one idea per note.

4. Have students share their notes in the center of the table and begin organizing them in clusters based on like attributes.

5. Once students are satisfied with the arrangement, have them label each cluster with a title that is representative of the grouping.

6. You might want to use the acronym *G.R.O.U.P.* to remember the steps in the process.

   G enerate data or gather it from another source

   R e-examine

   O rganize by similarities

   U se a label to identify groups

   P rocess and discuss

This is much more of a constructivist approach to concept attainment through participants' knowledge and personal input of generating data.

7. Sometimes participants may be given a data set and asked to organize it. They may not have the background to create data, or data is already available, and it wastes time to go through the generation process.

OTHER NOTES ■

These can be used in the following circumstances:

- Participants need some active involvement in constructing their own meaning
- Active involvement of personal ideas and kinesthetic task is needed
- Dialogue and creating understanding of concepts is necessary
- Need for dialogue and elaboration exists

Examples and Uses

1. This can be used to generate and come to consensus on classroom norms for the group to live by. Participants will generate things that are important to them as the group works together over time. These can be clustered and discussed, and several *norms* or *rules* to live by can be identified.

2. *What do you know about_____?* may be another prompt for which people can generate attributes. This also makes an easy pre-assessment to find out what a student already knows about a topic.

3. This can be used after students read a passage or piece of text to help build memory of facts and then sort those facts into categories. Analysis of facts early in learning and creating categories helps aid memory of newly learned material.

■ WHAT DO I KNOW ABOUT CANADA, EH?

Ask each person in the group to generate and/or brainstorm (one per sticky note) what he or she knows (or thinks he or she knows) about Canada.

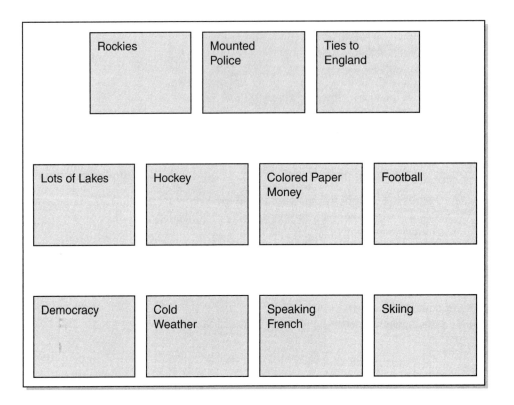

■ CLUSTERS AND CATEGORIES FOR STUDENTS' SORTED FACTS

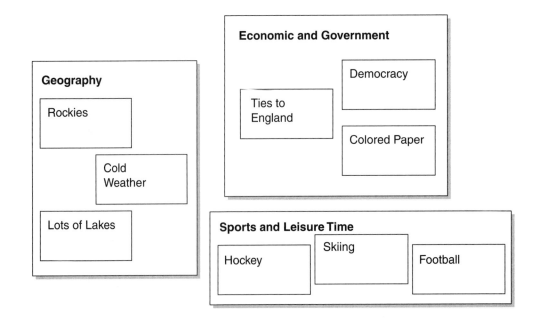

Ask each person in the group to generate (one per sticky note) several ways he or she likes to travel.

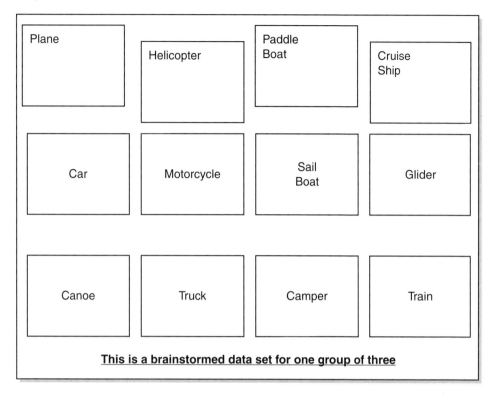

This is a brainstormed data set for one group of three

CLUSTERS AND CATEGORIES FOR STUDENTS SORTED FACTS ■

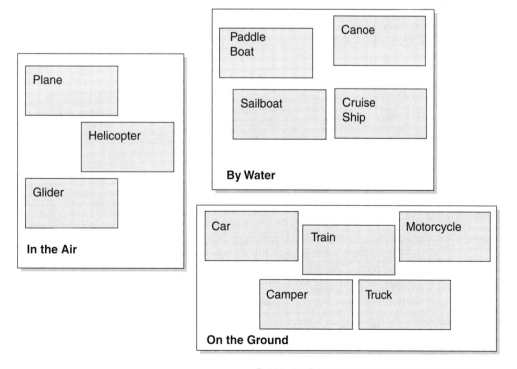

SELECTED REFERENCE ■

Taba (1967)

SHARING KNOWLEDGE AND SKILLS
Content Dialogue

■ PURPOSE AND DESCRIPTION

Content Dialogue is a strategy that helps students practice conversation and use of newly acquired concepts and ideas. Students do not come to us knowing how to dialogue about content. The tools in this section foster memory of newly learned material, help students connect to prior knowledge, extend their thinking and analysis about learning and learn that dialogue is a terrific study strategy. We know that dialogue-based rehearsal of content improves student thinking and learning. We know that students need structured conversations when first learning these skills. This strategy can be used in any content area and in most grades.

Making Connections

Brain Bits	This process emphasizes the impact of deeper thinking using collaborative learning and developing patterns and both verbal and visual connections. Learning to state content information in your own words is a key learning strategy and a study strategy that increases memory and analysis of new material.
Theaters of the Mind	Reflective, Social, Physical, and Cognitive Learning
Learning Styles	Beach Ball: creativity, Microscope: problem solving, Clipboard: process-based thinking, Puppy: processing, Interpersonal: sequential and random
Research Basis	Questioning, cues and advanced organizers, analysis, application, evaluation and synthesis, cooperative grouping, nonlinguistic representation, examples and nonexamples, visual metaphors, and summarization
Grouping	Use with groups of two students for the Q and A cards. Use with groups of three to five for sorting and analysis activity.
Grade Level	This technique works well for late elementary, middle level, and high school. For younger or less-literate students, use as a role-play in front of the class so the teacher can coach and then as a Think-Pair-Share.
Timing	Provide 10 to 30 minutes depending on the prompts and roles. Be certain to model use of the question-and-answer stems and the roles in the conversation. Use at the beginning of the unit for new learning or to build upon prior learning and review or extend it prior to assessment.

Other Notes	Prepare and walk through a model with students first.
	English language learners and some students with learning disabilities may need to see this rehearsed in front of the class in the form of role-plays several times before they can replicate it.
	Assign roles to start and demonstrate to students how to switch roles when you call time or indicate a switch of roles is needed.
	Assign criteria for reporting the final product and thinking of the group.
	This works well on abstract or new concepts as well as on controversial themes or ideas.
	Add additional questions as needed to deepen understanding through relevant application or examples.
	After practice, students can create their own question-and-answer cards; this is a good review strategy prior to assessment and a group study tool.

STEPS AND DIRECTIONS

1. Introduce students to new content, including relevant vocabulary. Use great strategies such as Concept Formation to help students remember the new ideas and vocabulary.

2. Give students the opportunity to read selections that use the new vocabulary or view film clips to provide additional background knowledge.

3. Use the Question and Answer Rehearsal Cards to help students work in pairs and practice the use of the new ideas in their structured dialogue.

4. As a review prior to a class assessment, have students create their own sets of Question and Answer Rehearsal Cards. Each team of three to five students can try their own set and then trade sets with other teams to enhance review of material. This also works well when rehearsing for state assessments or other high stakes tests.

SELECTED REFERENCES ■

Brock (1986), Buehl (1995), Feldman, Kinsella, and Stump (2002), Gregory and Kuzmich (2007), Harmin (1995), Kagan (1992a, 1992b), Long, Brock, Crookes, Deicke, Potter, and Zhang (1984), Rowe (1974), Vaughan and Estes (1986)

■ GENERAL EXAMPLES OF QUESTION AND ANSWER CARD REHEARSAL FOR MIDDLE AND HIGH SCHOOL

1. Use with pairs of students.

2. Give each a set of cards, all the questions or all the answer stems in order.

3. Have the first student ask the question on card one and the second student answer using the sentence stem on answer card one.

4. After two or three rounds, switch roles.

5. You can color code the answer versus the question card for easy sorting and storage.

6. Make up content specific sets for units of study.

Set One

Question Card 1:	Answer Card 1:
How could you sort all our new vocabulary words into like groups?	I would sort our words into the following groups . . . .

Set Two

Question Card 2:	Answer Card 2:
Which concept that we learned is the most important and why?	The most important concept is . . . because . . . .

Set Three

Question Card 3:	Answer Card 3:
After reading or viewing this information, where do you think we will be able to use this information?	We will be able to use this information . . . since . . . .

Set Four

Question Card 4:	Answer Card 4:
Under what circumstances do you think you can use this information?	I can use this information . . . .

CONTENT SPECIFIC EXAMPLES OF ■ QUESTION AND ANSWER CARD REHEARSAL FOR MIDDLE AND HIGH SCHOOL

Math Examples

Question Card:

Which problem-solving strategy worked best for you and why?

Answer Card:

I selected . . . strategy, because . . . .

Question Card:

What steps did you take to solve . . .?

Answer Card:

First, I . . . then I . . . finally, I . . . .

Science Examples:

Question Card:

How did you arrive at your hypothesis?

Answer Card:

I saw a pattern in how . . . reacted with . . . .

Question Card:

What conclusions did you draw from that experiment and why?

Answer Card:

I think that . . . based on the data that indicated . . . .

Social Studies Examples

Question Card:

Which causes for the war were the primary reason the conflict started and why?

Answer Card:

I think that the . . . caused . . . to respond in . . . way. So that caused the start of the war.

Question Card:

What was the author's purpose and how do you know this?

Answer Card:

I think that the author's purpose was . . . because . . . .

ELA Examples

Question Card:

What should we learn from the economic crisis of the depression? Does that apply today?

Answer Card:

I think that we should learn . . . .

It applies today since . . . .

Question Card:

What lesson can we learn from the two main characters that might help us with our friendships?

Answer Card:

The biggest lesson is . . . .
I think it helps with our friendships because . . . .

■ EXAMPLES OF QUESTION AND ANSWER CARD REHEARSAL FOR ELEMENTARY STUDENTS

Set One

1. Question Card: How do these two words go together?	1. Answer Card: _____ and _____ go together because . . . .

Set Two

2. Question Card: Why is this important to you or your family?	2. Answer Card: It is important because . . . .

Set Three

3. Question Card: Do you agree with. . . ?	3. Answer Card: Choose Yes or No Tell why . . . .

SMALL TEAMS OF THREE TO FIVE STUDENTS MAKING QUESTION AND ANSWER CARDS TO REVIEW FOR AN ASSESSMENT

This works for students in third grade and up.

1. Give students questions and answer stems to select from and encourage them to also make up their own.

2. Give students a critical list of vocabulary words, concepts, facts, or examples they need to remember for the assessment.

3. Have students develop a given number of sets of question and answer cards that are numbered as in our examples above.

4. Students can practice their own cards first and make any needed adjustments.

5. Give students a small resealable plastic bag, and place the questions and answer stems in the bag. Students can now trade bags with another team. The other team can report how they did and whether the question and answer stems were helpful.

OTHER NOTES

See the following stems and words (pp. 88–89) to help students and teachers create these Q-and-A cards. Please note that we provided stems and words at analysis, synthesis, and evaluation to increase rigorous thinking about content. As all classrooms are full of diverse learners, all students need to be able to develop and answer questions that build on their thinking. Students developing questions is an excellent check for understanding that enables teachers to assess depth of understanding and clarity of thought. This provides data for grouping and differentiating next steps or for reteaching.

Use or Create Question Stems or Prompts to Increase Rigor

Analysis

Which events could have happened . . . ?

If . . . happened, what might the ending have been?

How was this similar to . . . ?

What was the underlying theme of . . . ?

What do you see as other possible outcomes?

Why did . . . changes occur?

Can you compare your . . . with that presented in . . . ?

Can you explain what must have happened when . . . ?

How is . . . similar to . . . ?

What are some of the problems of . . . ?

Can you distinguish between . . . ?

What were some of the motives behind . . . ?

What was the turning point in the game?

What was the problem with . . . ?

Synthesis

Can you design a . . . to . . . ?

Why not compose a song about . . . ?

Can you see a possible solution to . . . ?

If you had access to all resources how would you deal with . . . ?

Why don't you devise your own way to deal with . . . ?

What would happen if . . . ?

How many ways can you . . . ?

Can you create new and unusual uses for . . . ?

Can you write a new recipe for a tasty dish?

Can you develop a proposal that would . . . ?

Evaluation

Is there a better solution to . . . ?

Judge the value of . . . .

Can you defend your position about . . . ?

Do you think . . . is a good or a bad thing?

How would you have handled . . . ?

What changes to . . . would you recommend?

Do you believe . . . ?

Are you a . . . person?

How would you feel if . . . ?

How effective are . . . ?

What do you think about . . . ?

More Words to Use:

Set standards for evaluating the following:

— which are good, bad?

— which one(s) do you like?

— what do you think are the most likely?

— rate from good to poor

— select and choose

— is that good or bad?

— weigh according to the standards

— judge by how you feel—what is the problem?

— are these solutions adequate?

— will it work?

— decide which . . . .

SELECTED REFERENCES ■

Bloom (1980), Bloom (1984), Dalton and Smith (1986)

Other Tools to Create Great Questions and Prompts

■ POWER WORDS

Analysis

Analyze	Discriminate	Monitor
Ask	Dissect	Observe
Catalog	Distinguish	Order
Categorize	Divide	Outline
Cause	Document	Point out
Chart	Edit	Problem
Classify	Examine	Proofread
Compare	Explain	Reason
Consequences of	Group	Review
Contract	How	Segment
Correlate	Identify	Sequence
Decode	Infer	Solution
Deduce	Inquire	Sort survey
Diagram	Inspect	Transform
Differentiate	Inventory	Why

More words to use for analysis:

- — what are the causes
- — what are the consequences
- — what are the steps in the process
- — how would you start
- — arrange
- — specify the conditions
- — which are necessary for
- — which one comes first, last
- — what are some specific examples of
- — list all the problems, solutions
- — distinguish one from another

Synthesis

Adopt	Devise	Integrate
Arrange	Dictate	Interact
Assemble	Elaborate	Invent
Blend	Establish	Make
Build	Explain	Model
Collect	Form	Organize
Combine	Format	Participate
Compile	Formulate	Plan
Compose	Frame	Portray
Concoct	Gather	Publish
Connect	Generate	Rearrange
Construct	Glean	Refine
Create	Graph	Revise
Cultivate	Hypothesis formation	Suppose
Design	Image	Synthesize
Develop	Incorporate	Write

More words to use for synthesis:

— how many hypotheses can you suggest

— think of all the different ways

— how else

— what would happen if

— think of as many as you can

— what would it be like if

— how many ways are possible

— in what ways can you improve

— form a new

— think of something no one else has thought of before

Evaluation

Adequacy	Determine	Perceive
Agree	Discriminate	Prioritize
Agreement	Dispute	Pros and cons
Appraise	Editorialize	Prove
Appreciate	Estimate	Rate
Assess	Evaluate	Reconsider
Choose	Explain	Recommend
Compare	Grade	Refute
Conclude	Hypothesize	Select
Consider	Importance	Set standards
Contrast	Influence	Support
Criticize	Interpret	Sustainability
Critique	Judge	Test
Debate	Justify	Value
Decide basis	Measure	Verify
Decide which	Most likely	Weigh
Defend	Opinion	

More words to use for evaluation:

Set standards for evaluating the following

— which are good, bad?

— which one(s) do you like?

— what do you think are the most likely?

— rate from good to poor

— select and choose

— is that good or bad?

— weigh according to the standards

— judge by how you feel

— what is the problem?

— are these solutions adequate?

— will it work

— decide which

Source: Adapted from ProTeacher Web site, for more information, see http://www.proteacher.com/

More Stems for Questions or Prompts

Other Analysis Stems:

How can you distinguish between_____?

How is (are) ___connected to ___?

How would you compare ___?

How would you document ___?

How would you monitor _____?

How would you order (put in order) _____?

What assumptions can you make and/or were made about _____?

What can you infer _____?

What can you point out about ___ that is significant?

What conclusions can you deduce ___?

What evidence can you list _____?

What evidence will support/refute _____?

What fallacies are found in _____?

What ideas validate _____?

What impact _____?

What inferences can you make _____?

What is the relationship between _____ and _____?

What is your analysis of _____?

What was the turning point _____?

What were some of the motives behind _____?

Why do you think _____?

Other Synthesis Stems:

Develop an investigation to determine ___.

Devise a way to _____.

Elaborate on _____.

How could you integrate _____ and _____?

How might you modify _____ to better _____?

How could you ___the plan ___?

How could you write a ___ about ___?

How would you compose _____?

How would you design a/an ____ that would change ____?

How would you formulate ____?

How would you generate a plan ____?

How could you portray ____?

Develop or propose a hypothesis for ____?

If you could ___, what would ___? Why?

Think of an original way to ___.

What alternatives would you suggest for ___?

How would you revise ____ to ___?

What could be modified to ___?

What could you invent to ___?

What solutions would you suggest ___?

What theory can you develop about ___?

Other Evaluation Stems:

Hypothesize the reason for ____.

Based on the evidence, explain why you chose ___.

Defend (Justify, Rationalize, Refute, Recommend) ____. Why are you choosing this viewpoint?

Do you agree with the outcome of ___? Why?

How might you check that ___ is really ___?

How would you critique ____?

How would you decide ___? Explain your thinking.

How would you determine which facts had the most impact on ___?

How would you grade ___?

How would you prove ___?

Justify your interpretation of ___.

Rank or rate ___. Justify the ranking or rating.

What choice would you have made ___? Why?

What data was used to evaluate ___? Why?

What information would you use to prioritize ___?

Which is more important, ___ or ___? Defend your response.

SHARING KNOWLEDGE AND SKILLS
Note Taking and Summarizing

PURPOSE   ■

Note taking and summarizing are key skills in learning to learn. It increases active involvement with content and fosters higher-order thinking skills. It creates a record for review and study purposes. It is a way to organize and process data to increase long-term retention and comprehension.

DESCRIPTION   ■

To effectively take quality notes, students need to be able to select key information, delete irrelevant information, and substitute some information. Information should be organized in a meaningful way that increases student understanding and long-term memory. This can be accomplished using a variety of tools. In a differentiated classroom, we want to provide students with a variety of methods supporting differences in visual and verbal learners.

Making Connections

Brain Bits	Seek meaning, relevancy and connections. Looking for patterns and increasing long-term memory.
Theaters of the Mind	Reflective, Cognitive, and Social Learning
Learning Styles	Microscope: visual learning
Research Basis	Questioning, cues and advanced organizers, note taking and summarizing
Grouping	Use with one, two, or three student groups
Grade Level	This technique works for elementary, middle level, and high school.
Timing	Before, during, and after learning
Other Notes	Ask questions during group processing to support checking assumptions, author's point of view, and inferential thinking.

STEPS AND DIRECTIONS

1. To summarize effectively, students need to be able to perform three operations:
   - Delete unnecessary information
   - Substitute some information
   - Keep key information (Kintsch, 1974; van Dijk, 1980)

2. To perform these operations takes deep thinking and analysis.

3. Tools are helpful in doing this thinking, identification, and analysis.

In the 1950s, Walter Pauk, an education professor at Cornell University, created the *Cornell Note Taking System.* Part of this system suggested that students do the following:

1. *Record*: During the lecture, record any key information.

2. *Reduce*: After class, ideas and facts are concisely summarized to clarify understanding, connections, and reinforce memory.

3. *Recite*: Dialogue strengthens and clarifies concepts. This helps to transfer the facts and ideas to the long-term memory.

4. *Reflect*: The student's reaction and reflection helps the brain recall and restore information. Accessing, examining, and refiling information adds to the memory process.

5. *Review*: Student should review the notes regularly. Key information is recalled more easily the more it is accessed and examined.

Source: Adapted from *How to Study in College* by Walter Pauk, 2001, Houghton Mifflin Company.

■ OTHER NOTES

The process of summarizing and taking notes is a key skill in recording new information or reviewing information to which students have already been exposed.

The brain uses the writing and review process to deepen understanding and create memorable notations. Students should be exposed to numerous ways to record key information and reflect on the ways that create stronger memory hooks for them.

QCR NOTE TAKING   ■

One way of note taking would be to use an organizer that would help students focus on key ideas and make connections.

1. Using the center column, record key ideas from text or from what was said.

2. As questions arise, place in left-hand column.

3. Jot down connections and reflections in the right-hand column.

Questions	Content	Reflections

■ **QCR EXAMPLE: AFRICAN AMERICAN MUSICIANS: JAZZ**

Questions	Content	Reflections
What types of music typify each decade?	20th century music Jazz was a great musical influence. Ragtime developed by Scott Joplin in 1890's preceded jazz. Syncopation was a technique that evolved where an accented beat follows an unaccented beat.	I had no idea it was so influential.
In which cities did jazz originate?	Ragtime beat was consistent, but jazz is played differently with the right and left hands. Jelly Roll Morton invented jazz in 1902 in New Orleans. Duke Ellington shaped jazz through original compositions. He wrote to the strength of his musicians and allowed for improvisational styles. Ragtime Joplin Jazz: Improv Jelly Roll Ellington	This was quite interesting and must be challenging to do. I'd like to listen to more jazz by famous artists.
Summary:		

Questions can be developed using the prompts from Bloom's Taxonomy or Quellmalz's Thinking Taxonomy.

USING BLOOM'S TAXONOMY AS A NOTE TAKER   ▪

This chart can be used to encourage students to process new content in an in-depth way.

Level of Thinking	Questions	Notes
Recall	List the information you have identified as key.	
Comprehension	Summarize the main ideas.	
Application	With a partner, discuss the key ideas.	
Analysis	What is a key question related to the main ideas?	
Synthesis	Draw a word web that connects the main ideas.	
Evaluation	What conclusions and reactions do you have related to this content?	

■ QUELLMALZ'S THINKING TAXONOMY

This note taker may be used for processing content (declarative knowledge). The following chart may be used as a guide to peruse main idea.

Level	Definition	Trigger Words
Recall Information	Evidence of content	Paraphrase Retell Repeat Restate Express in another form
Analysis Whole to parts	Dividing into parts Characteristics and/or sequence may be part of analysis	Relationships Cause and effect Sequencing
Comparison Similarities and/or differences	Focus on details	Similarities Differences Analogies Metaphors
Inference General implications	Draw conclusions by combining and drawing generalities	Hypothesizing Predicting Concluding Synthesizing Deducing Inferring
Evaluation Making judgment	Judging the quality and/or credibility using criteria and justifying rationale	Explaining Rationalizing Giving evidence Assembling Justification
Summary of the most important ideas from your notes:		

K.I.M. NOTE TAKER ■

This note-taking method works well for vocabulary words and the introduction of new concepts. *K* = Key Word, *I* = Information about the word (often using other content vocabulary) and *M* = a Memory strategy.

Key Word	Information about the Word	Memory Strategy: (Mnemonics, Pictures, Clipart)
Write a definition in your own words using the K.I.M. notes:		

Writing a definition in your own words is an excellent summary strategy and increases the probability you will remember the word and connections that explain the word.

K = Key Word or Concept	I = Information or data	M = Memory Strategy
Animal cells versus plant cells	Cell wall difference Replication Cell structures and functions Why are cells important? Controversial issues	
Write a summary or definition in your own words:		

K = Key Word or Concept	I = Information or data	M = Memory Strategy
Communism	Economic system Redistribution of wealth Social system Run by a Totalitarian government	
My definition: Communism is a social and economic system of organization based on the holding of the equal distribution of property and money, controlled by a central government.		

THE 5-W NOTE TAKER ■

Some note taking is facilitated using the media model of 5-W. The following chart may be used to capture key information and reactions and/or illustrations.

Criteria	Key Points	Illustrations/Diagrams
Who?		
What?		
Where?		
When?		
How?		

Using Graphic Organizers as Note Takers

Using a graphic organizer will also help learners discuss, process, and record key information. Follow up the use of any graphic organizer with a writing prompt to summarize the information, put definitions in the student's own words, or draw conclusions. Here are three organizers that work well for this purpose.

■ CONCEPT MAP

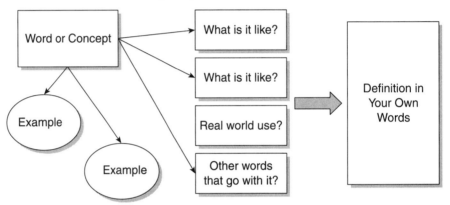

Concept Map—One Possible Version

■ VENN DIAGRAM

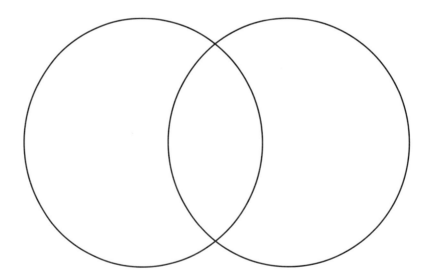

Add a prompt to a Venn Diagram that allows students to create a summary of the most important similarities, differences, or both. You can also use three or four circles to do larger comparisons for older students or learners who can handle more complex thinking in a differentiated classroom.

FISHBONE

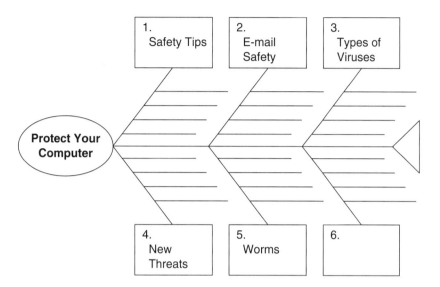

SHARING KNOWLEDGE AND SKILLS

Wallpaper Poster

■ PURPOSE AND DESCRIPTION

Wallpaper Poster is a group comprehension strategy that supports summarizing and analysis for deeper understanding of complex concepts as students are just introduced to the learning through articles, Internet, video, real world documents, or text. This strategy allows teachers to pay attention to more learning styles going beyond verbal and linguistic to visual spatial. We also want students to summarize and clearly state information in precise ways. This increases application of the concept, long-term memory, and helps students connect new learning to prior learning. This provides a satisfying learning experience for visual, auditory, tactile and/or kinesthetic learners in a differentiated classroom.

Making Connections

Brain Bits	This process emphasizes the impact of deeper thinking using collaborative learning and developing patterns and both verbal and visual connections. Learning to restate information in your own words and nonlinguistic representation are key learning strategies that use more of the brain for processing and thereby increase memory and application of new material.
Theaters of the Mind	Reflective, Social, Physical, and Cognitive Learning
Learning Styles	Beach Ball: creativity, Microscope: problem solving, Clipboard: process-based thinking, Puppy: processing, Interpersonal: sequential and random
Research Basis	Questioning, cues and advanced organizers, analysis, application, evaluation and synthesis, cooperative grouping, nonlinguistic representation, examples and nonexamples, visual metaphors, and summarization
Grouping	Use with groups of two students if you use the larger paper graphic organizers or groups up to six if you use chart paper. Groups of two could also create an electronic version that can be projected for the class as the groups report out.
Grade Level	This technique works well for late elementary, middle level, and high school. For younger or less-literate students, use as a shared writing opportunity with students coming up to report on each aspect of a large group poster.
Timing	Provide 10 to 30 minutes depending on the prompts and roles. Be certain to model use of the questions and the roles in the conversation technique to develop the poster as well as to report out the results.

Use at the beginning of the unit for new learning or to build upon prior learning and review or extend it. |

Other Notes	Prepare and walk through a model with students first.
	English language learners and some students with learning disabilities may need leveled written material if you are using this technique for new learning or for processing information.
	Assign roles creating the posters.
	Assign roles for reporting out the final product and thinking of the group.
	This works well on abstract or new concepts as well as controversial themes or ideas.
	Add additional questions as needed to deepen understanding through relevant application or examples. Only add one or two more questions depending on difficulty to stay in the time range for this activity.
	After practice, students can create their own posters from a selection of optional and nonoptional questions and prompts. Students could also create their own questions based on what they think fellow students need to know and be taught.
	If each group created a different poster about multiple concepts being taught, this would make a great jigsaw activity. See jigsaw.

STEPS AND DIRECTIONS

1. Have participants read an article or perhaps view a video noting the key points.

2. You could ask different groups to attend to different topics.

3. Have partners or small groups place the topic on the top of a piece of chart paper. (You can also use the idea of a "mini" poster and put the template on a piece of copy paper for pairs to use, suggest 8.5 by 14 inch to give more room or even construction paper size to simulate the idea of a concept poster.)

4. Next, people will define the concept in their own words.

5. Then, create a symbol to represent the concept visually. Five students use colorful markers or pencils to do this work.

6. Next, give examples that support the idea and be able to rationalize them.

7. Add any questions that help increase relevance and application; this helps students deepen understanding and increase memory.

8. Present to another small group (if you use the template as a conventional graphic organizer) or entire group (if you use chart paper).

SELECTED REFERENCES ∎

Beaudoin and Taylor (2004), Chang and Dalziel (1999a, 1999b), Erickson (2005), Gregory and Kuzmich (2007), Gregory, Robbins, and Herndon (2000), Hoffman and Olson-Ness (1996), Marzano (2004), Taba (1967), Wald and Castleberry (2000)

■ EXAMPLE OF WALLPAPER POSTER

Wallpaper Poster

Record the title on the top of the chart paper.

1. Define the concept (key ideas).

2. Design a symbol for the concept.

3. Give examples for the concept. Be prepared to state your rationale for selection.

SOURCE: Illustration from *Teacher Teams That Get Results* by Gregory and Kuzmich, 2007

■ OTHER NOTES

1. The teacher can add one or two additional questions such as the relevance or application of the concept, other uses, examples, or an alternative definition that depends on context.

2. Follow-up can include oral presentation of the work and/or a written summary in paragraph format.

EXAMPLE OF WALLPAPER POSTER TEMPLATE ■

Use on large chart paper for ease of reporting to rest of class (for groups of 4 to 6 students), or create a graphic organizer to help students work in pairs or triads. You can also create electronic posters or a slide show of your poster.

Place Concept or Theme or Issues Here
1. Define the concept in the title of this poster in your own words, using key ideas about this concept.
2. Draw a symbol that represents or helps you remember this concept.
3. Give an example of this type of concept. Why did you pick this example?
4. Add other questions here to deepen understanding and increase memory through relevancy and application.

■ SECONDARY EXAMPLE FOR MATH

Quadratic Equations
1. Define *Quadratic Equation* in your own words, using key ideas about type of equation.
2. Draw a symbol that represents or helps you remember Quadratic Equations. (Don't write an equation. What does it remind you of instead?)
3. Give an example of this type of equation. Why did you pick this particular equation?
4. How is this type of equation used in the real world, and who might use this type of math?

Note the addition of a relevancy question that helps students remember more about the concept and increases longer-term retrieval of the big ideas about the concept.

MIDDLE LEVEL EXAMPLE OF ISSUE OR ■
THEME-BASED LEARNING: STOP BULLYING

Stop Bullying
1. Define *Bullying* in your own words, using key ideas about type of behavior.
2. Draw a symbol or picture that represents or helps you remember how to prevent bullying or how to get help.
3. Give three examples of how to stop bullying. Why did you pick these particular solutions?
4. What should you personally do if you see or experience bullying?
5. How can adults in your world help you avoid bullying or bullies?

■ ELEMENTARY EXAMPLE FOR SOCIAL STUDIES

Community
1. Define *Community* in your own words, using key ideas about types of communities.
2. Draw a picture of a community. You can draw your own community.
3. Give an example of a community that is not your own. Why did you pick that kind of community?
4. Why are communities important?
5. How do communities help people live?

4

Integrating and Applying Learning

Introduction

Student teams are powerful in providing numerous benefits for learning and achievement. We often use teams to learn new things or share knowledge; however, students teams are also useful for applying learning and extending thinking and integration of knowledge. Students need to be able to do more than demonstrate comprehension; they need to use what they learn to make connections, solve problems, make decisions, and to create new ideas, processes, and products. Group work and interaction enables students to move more readily from receiving knowledge to generating knowledge then to using and integrating that knowledge for further critical thinking and learning. We know that through task-oriented dialogue, students are able to personalize knowledge and scaffold their thinking processes, rehearse more, and develop deeper understanding about what they are learning than they could individually. Cooperative learning teams paired with specific tasks and tools to accomplish those tasks have a powerful impact on assessment results, products, and thinking.

Integrating and sharing knowledge is also imperative in a differentiated classroom where flexible grouping based on readiness, interest, and learning profiles is encouraged and compacting is in place for students who advance quickly through the curriculum. Compacting (Renzulli, 1994)—enrichment or high challenge—is necessary when students grasp and understand the concepts and skills more quickly and need a robust thinking application. They should not be required to repeat learning activities that other learners may still need to develop understanding.

Most experts on team-based learning define it as a variety of strategies for enhancing the value of student-student dialogue-based interaction. In one well-known publication on cooperative learning (Johnson, Johnson, & Holubec, 1993), key benefits include the following:

KEY BENEFITS OF TEAM LEARNING	
Positive Interdependence	The feeling among a group of students that they need one another to be successful has been shown to positively impact a student's achievement and attitude toward learning.
Individual Accountability	The feeling among a group that each member is responsible for their own learning as well as that of their fellow students improves overall performance of both the group and the individuals in the group.
Collaborative Skills	These skills are lifelong and include the ability to see and benefit from multiple points of view, levels of understanding, and sharing of thinking through proactive communication.
Evaluation of Group Interaction	Time spent for groups to self-evaluate and process how well they have collaborated and how to enhance their future collaboration creates a realistic application of adapting to circumstances based on feedback.
Heterogeneous Grouping	Students working with students who are different from them on such variables as sex, past achievement, ethnicity, expertise, and/or knowledge, style, and persistence and/or motivation tend to gain more in achievement and have an increase in positive attitudes and persistence.

Putting these six benefits together creates a dynamic for learning that is hard to beat. In order to use what we learn, student teams consolidate thinking more rapidly than any individual could accomplish and also help make more intricate connections that lead to applying what we learn for solutions, creative inventions, and flexible decision making. This type of social interaction helps us rehearse for life, work, and lifelong learning since it requires higher levels of cognitive complexity than individual learning can accomplish.

In a study by Gruenfeld and Hollingshead in 1993, *Sociocognition in Work Groups: The Evolution of Group Integrative Complexity and Its Relation to Task Performance*, individual achievement and critical thinking were compared to achievement with group processing. The study examined the integration of complex thinking about multiple concepts that were learned when shared in a group culture. The researchers looked at how individual group member's thinking can impact both task and performance of the entire group over time. So the conclusions support that the group enhances individual performance more and more over time. The findings in this study using individual and group writing quality and complexity support the developing notion that thoughts and ideas can be conceived as collective in a team, rather than a purely individual task.

There is also some additional and outstanding research outside and inside of PreK–12 education on the role of discourse and social interaction that benefits thinking. On behalf of NATO and an international conference on cognition and learning, Lauren Resnick (1997), a professor at the University of Pittsburgh, edited a wonderful summary of this research with findings from the fields of the following:

- Psychology
- Education
- Sociology
- Artificial intelligence
- Linguistics
- Anthropology

These studies examine how people think and learn in settings as diverse as a factory, a classroom, or an airplane cockpit. The tools that people use in these varied settings are both physical technologies and cultural constructions: concepts, structures of reasoning, and forms of discourse. All of the studies indicated the same conclusions:

- Interactive dialogue grounds reasoning.
- When tools are used to organize the team effort, learning results.
- Learning deeply requires someone to join a community for practice, application, and cognition.

In conventional educational research for PreK–12 learning, cooperative learning is believed to promote thinking and creativity in many ways (Hythecker, Dansereau, & Rocklin, 1988; Qin, Johnson, & Johnson, 1995; Webb, 1989), including the following:

1. In cooperative learning, students have more opportunities to talk and to share ideas than in whole-group situations. This interaction with students encourages students to restructure their ideas. For instance, they may need to summarize, elaborate, exemplify, defend, and explain their ideas in their own words.

2. Students clarify and rethink their ideas to get agreement or common understanding among team members, potentially leading to cognitive restructuring.

3. Students get to see how their peers think and create new ideas. Witnessing this process can provide useful models, and then emulating peers results in needed practice for deeper cognition and long-term memory.

4. If students feel positively interdependent with one another, a supportive atmosphere can develop. In such an atmosphere, students may feel freer to try out new, more creative ideas when less anxiety or risk is present.

5. The multiple perspectives of others in diverse groups may trigger new ideas in students' minds. Heterogeneous groups are much better for learning than homogeneous groupings.

6. Research clearly indicates that greater achievement is possible with cooperative learning and it can provide students with a stronger knowledge base from which to explore more complex concepts. Thus, in a differentiated classroom with diverse learners, heterogeneous cooperative groups enhance and deepen thinking and understanding for all students. If I don't know too much, I learn from those who know more. If I know a lot, I clarify my own thinking through explanations and verbal rehearsal. If I am an English Language Learner, I hear and use vocabulary and develop sentence patterns in a safe and supportive way. (Adapted from Tan, G., Gallo, P., Jacobs, G., & Lee, C., 1999)

Marzano, Pickering, and Pollack (2001), in *Classroom Instruction That Works*, noted that while cooperative learning has been around for a long time in education, military, work, and community applications, additional studies have shown the benefits of student teams to increase critical thinking, quality of learning products, and creativity in solutions. The following section of this book has seven powerful strategies for maximizing the benefits of social interaction and pairing it with equally powerful thinking tools and graphic organizers so that students can take their learning to the next level of creativity and integration. Cooperative group learning (over 200 studies) has an effect size of .73 with an associated percentile gain on standardized assessments of 27, and advanced organizers paired with questions and cues (over 300 studies on various types of graphic organizers) have an effect size of .59 with an associated percentile gain on standardized assessments of 22. Think of it this way: students who learn in cooperative groups have higher assessment results than 76% of their peers who learned the same material individually, and students who use graphic organizers score better than 73% of peers who do not use organizers with questions and cues or organizers of any kind.

When we combine both of these highly effective and research-based methods, the results in achievement and attitude are remarkable and even persistence for tasks improves. We feel strongly that any learning organization that wants results for diverse students and needs to rapidly close any achievement gaps should seriously consider these approaches. We hope that some of our suggestions give you ideas for adding additional research-based practices to these selected methods we found to be especially powerful. We have also included notes on differentiation and technology integration in several of the strategies. We know that critical thinking requires differentiation in terms of scaffolding, relevance, resources, and results. These strategies are designed to give teachers ways to do that easily with these strategies. We want your students to achieve more with better attitudes and greater persistence. The strategies we included only take from 10 to 60 minutes and can be used for a variety of levels and courses. We also want to increase the application and memory of what you teach and the ability of each student to integrate that learning enough to use it for deeper critical thinking, connect it with known learning, and use it to adapt to new circumstances and more complex learning. They are also essential in a differentiated classroom as they provide a variety of ways for students with diverse readiness, interest, and learning profiles.

■ PURPOSEFUL TEAMING

We used these criteria as we developed the strategies in this section of the book. We feel strongly that well-rehearsed process and communication, are worth time teaching and practicing, and skills should be reviewed with each grouping opportunity. By paying close attention to the criteria for successful, flexible, and cooperative groups, we can achieve better integration and application of learning at higher levels of critical thinking:

- Demonstrate the application of knowledge
- Set goals for learning and results
- Learn strategies and study skills to promote long-term memory
- Develop the ability to generalize and use the organization of content for better critical thinking
- Generate hypotheses, test them, and draw justifiable conclusions
- Demonstrate effective critical-thinking skills
- Analyze issues, data, problems, processes, and products of learning to determine next steps and inferences
- Demonstrate effective problem-solving strategies
- Demonstrate creativity in group work and products or processes
- Demonstrate successful contributions to the team when the integration and thinking behind the content becomes challenging

We hope you find that these teaming strategies effectively build teams that are ready to learn and contribute to each other's success in your differentiated classroom. These critical-thinking strategies in a group context help students rehearse and develop the habits they will need for future success.

INTEGRATING AND APPLYING LEARNING

Four Squares for Creativity

PURPOSE AND DESCRIPTION ■

This method helps student teams look at ideas or issues from a new angle, expand the possibilities or solutions to a problem, and analyze the impact of possible solutions. The focus on creativity helps learners deepen thinking and increase the probability of success. This graphic organizer is an excellent tool for developing the fluid and flexible thought patterns essential to innovative thinking, reasoning, elaboration, generalization, and creativity.

The teacher must pose a question, or an older student team can choose or write a question that deals with issues, problems, points of view, solutions, dilemmas, controversy, or a hypothesis. This method works well toward the end of a unit and may help teachers evaluate the integration of student thinking about the content. It works well to scaffold student critical reflection in preparation for a performance assessment or even as a culminating piece in a unit.

Making Connections

Brain Bits	This process emphasizes the reflective learning system; students think more critically and creatively when given the opportunity to question and analyze a topic deeply. Supports social and active learning and gives students access to new ideas and the opportunity to integrate the new learning with the old.
Theaters of the Mind	Reflective and Cognitive Learning
Learning Styles	Beach Ball: creativity, Puppy: processing, Interpersonal: random
Research Basis	Questioning, cues and advanced organizers, nonlinguistic representation, using similarities and differences, analogies and metaphors, summarizing and note taking, cooperative learning, generating hypothesis, and cognitive complexity
Grouping	Use with groups of two or three students.
Grade Level	This technique works for late elementary, middle level, and high school. For younger or less-literate students, this could be used as a whole-group discussion tool to model this type of thinking.
Timing	Provide 45 to 60 minutes with prior modeling by teacher. Use with very small groups toward the end of the unit or for a formative assessment during the unit.
Other Notes	Ask questions during group processing to support originality and creativity. What if . . . how could we . . .why not . . . and so on work well to coach teams.

STEPS AND DIRECTIONS

1. Review the purpose for this activity in terms of establishing priority and looking at the problem, issue, or topic from a new perspective.

2. Model the process using a well-understood, relevant tissue such as behavioral expectations or homework routines as examples.

3. Brainstorm aspects of the problem or process in question such as contributing factors or possible solutions.

4. Ask each small group to select one aspect off the brainstormed list.

5. Use the template to fully think through the issue or topic selected.

6. Share one or more four squares with total group if you have six or fewer small groups. With more small groups, pair groups after the templates are complete and share. Ask these groups to share common viewpoints.

7. Gather templates and use to report back on priorities for next steps or possible viewpoints that further the solution to a problem.

■ SELECTED REFERENCES

Gregory and Kuzmich (2005a, 2005b).

FOUR SQUARES FOR CREATIVITY ■

Topic or Prompt:_____

List as many facts or things you know about the topic as you can in five minutes. Use brainstorming rules. *Fluency*	How would other people feel about this topic? Given a specific audience convince others of your point of view. *Flexibility*

Originality
 	
1. Think of a new point of view about the topic.
2. Name your point of view
   _____
3. What will it help us do or think?
   _____
   _____
4. Draw a symbol for your point of view or new idea:
	Elaboration
	
	Describe your point of view or new idea as if it were an advertisement or editorial on the Internet or in the newspaper. Give it a level of importance or priority.

■ FOUR SQUARES FOR CREATIVITY

Subject: Technical Reading

Level: Grades 4 through 6

Prompt: What kind of tool is best for the purpose of a gift? Read ads, Web sites, consumer, or other related technical reading sources or articles prior to this activity.

List as many uses for a tool as you can in five minutes. Use brainstorming rules. Tool _____ *Fluency*	What kind of tools do you think your parents would like as a gift? You can guess. *Flexibility*
Originality Think of a new tool that everyone needs. Name your tool _____ What will it help us do? _____ _____ Draw your tool.	*Elaboration* Describe your tool so that we could use the description in an advertisement on the Internet or in the newspaper.

FOUR SQUARES FOR CREATIVITY ■

Subject: Technical Reading

Level: Grades 7 through 12

Prompt: What kind of communication method is best for communicating controversial ideas in this course? Which ones will work for your peers? Read ads, Web sites, view commercials, read consumer or other related technical reading sources or articles prior to this activity.

List multiple tools or methods of communicating controversial ideas in (list course) _____. Tools and methods for communication *Fluency*	What kind of tools or methods do you think would be most persuasive for your peers? Choose the methods that have the greatest chance of convincing others to adopt your point of view. Your peers? Your parents? Your employer or a community member? *Flexibility*
Originality Think of a new method of communication or vehicle for communication. What is it? Name your method _____ How will it help us communicate and persuade others when it comes to controversial topics? Draw or illustrate your idea	*Elaboration* Describe your tool or method so that we could use the description in an advertisement on the Internet or in the school newspaper

INTEGRATING AND APPLYING LEARNING

Point of View

■ PURPOSE

This is a great process for sorting solutions and making decisions. Understanding the pros and cons and advantages and disadvantages all help students to select the best solutions by weighing evidence, points of view, and other data sources. Inviting students to do this prior to summarizing, solving problems, selecting solutions, prioritizing, and making final decisions is a life skill. It helps students rehearse complex evaluation by integrating information, viewpoint, and analysis skills. These graphic organizers used in small groups can help teachers scaffold student thinking in evaluation, synthesis, and analysis.

Making Connections

Brain Bits	This process emphasizes the brain's need to make connections, pay attention to meaningful information and irrelevant information, act upon curiosity, and collaborate to solve complex problems or issues.
Theaters of the Mind	Reflective and Cognitive Learning
Learning Styles	Clipboard: data organization, Microscope: analysis, Puppy: processing, Beach Ball: curiosity, Interpersonal: sequential
Research Basis	Questioning, cues and advanced organizers, nonlinguistic representation, using similarities and differences, generating hypotheses and questions, metacognition
Grouping	Use with groups of two or three students.
Grade Level	This technique works for late elementary, middle level, and high school. For younger or less-literate students this could be used as a whole-group discussion tool to model this type of thinking.
Timing	Provide 10 to 20 minutes with prior modeling by teacher and prior reading or gathering of information. Use with very small groups toward the end of the unit or for a formative assessment during the unit.
Other Notes	Ask questions during group processing to support deep analysis thinking about similarities and differences, compare and contrast, and cause and effect. Learners with special needs or English Language Learners may require a word bank, their notes, or visual cues if this process includes a large quantity of newly learned content vocabulary. You will need one of the graphic organizers on a sheet of paper, a piece of a chart paper or have students make a T-chart or two-flap foldable with labels from one of the organizers on the flaps or columns.

STEPS AND DIRECTIONS

1. Given a problem or goal that a group is going to tackle, use any of the brainstorming techniques to develop a list of possible solutions. Teacher provides or student develops a key question. A question that is essential but may have multiple points of view and answers. A key question is never a yes or no question and is always at the analysis, synthesis, or evaluation level.

2. Take each of the solutions and analyze them as to one of the following:
   - Pros and Cons
   - Pluses and Minuses (use instead of Pros and Cons if desired)
   - Advantages and Disadvantages
   - Benefits and Hindrances

3. Discuss which solutions have benefits that outweigh negative or roadblock issues. These are the solutions the group can incorporate at the start of a project, individual writing, assessment, or other complex demonstration of learning.

SELECTED REFERENCES ■

Beaudoin and Taylor (2004), Burke (1993), Chadwick (2006), Chang and Buster (1999), Costa and Garmston (2002), Daniels (1986), Deal and Peterson (1998, 2002), Gregory and Kuzmich (2005a, 2005b), Gregory and Kuzmich (2007), Johnson, Johnson, and Smith (1991b), Roberts and Pruitt (2003)

■ POINT OF VIEW

Template Ideas:

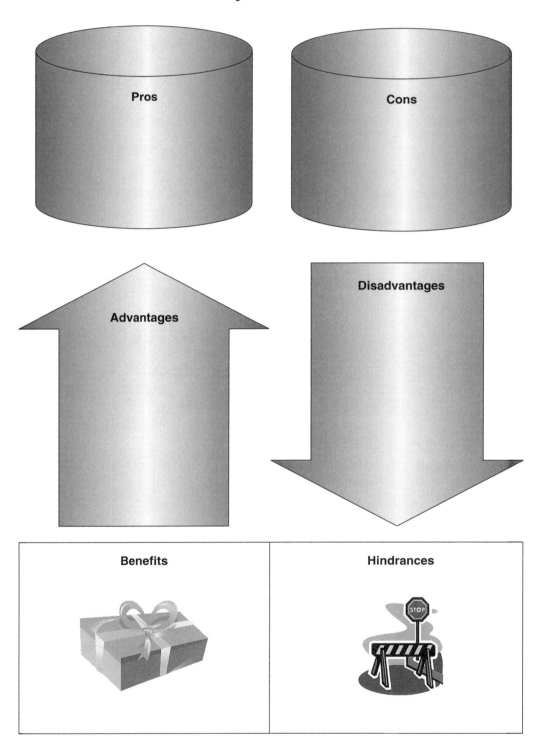

ELEMENTARY EXAMPLES ■

Pros and Cons

Example of a Key Question: Math

What are the pros and cons of using a drawing to solve a math problem?

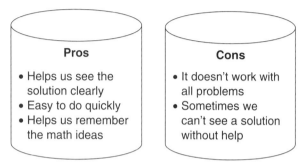

Pros

- Helps us see the solution clearly
- Easy to do quickly
- Helps us remember the math ideas

Cons

- It doesn't work with all problems
- Sometimes we can't see a solution without help

INTERMEDIATE, MIDDLE, OR ■ HIGH SCHOOL EXAMPLE

Advantages and Disadvantages

Example of a Key Question: Social Issues

Is it ever OK to tease a younger person?

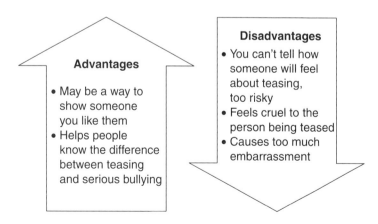

Advantages

- May be a way to show someone you like them
- Helps people know the difference between teasing and serious bullying

Disadvantages

- You can't tell how someone will feel about teasing, too risky
- Feels cruel to the person being teased
- Causes too much embarrassment

■ HIGH SCHOOL EXAMPLE

Benefits and Hindrances

Example of a Key Question: Science

Is stem cell research warranted?

Benefits	Hindrances

• Potential for curing many diseases that are the result of accidents or wars	• Religious objections by some groups who feel this entire line of research is related to taboo issues or unborn fetuses
• Many sources of stem cells now, not just fetus tissue	• Complex and expensive research
• Economic benefit to our country for research and development, marketing of successful research and cures	• May or may not lead to cures
• Personal and social benefit of ending suffering in everything from cancer to spinal cord injuries and diseases like Parkinson's Disease	• Continued public misunderstanding about what it is and what it isn't
• Puts United States in a good position with the rest of the world in this type of research and our standards for marketable cures and solutions are very high	• Does the means outweigh the end results, currently this is a moral dilemma in the debate rather than a scientific argument or process

INTEGRATING AND APPLYING LEARNING
iREAP

PURPOSE AND DESCRIPTION ■

iREAP is a process of deepening thinking by looking at the same piece of text or source of information from multiple points of view. The process encourages learners to revisit information and check their assumptions before inferring or creating conclusion. This type of thinking is a valuable life skill. The graphic organizer for iREAP is useful with fiction and non-fiction prose as well as document (nonprose charts, maps, graphs, etc.) or technological resources.

This graphic organizer will help students deepen understanding of text, research, Web site, media, and other information sources. This method of rehearsal will assist students to perform better on assessments that ask questions or require tasks that are related to analytic thought, complex decision making or problem solving, defending a point of view, checking assumptions, synthesis, and evaluation.

Other ways to use this graphic organizer with small groups of students or as an individual assessment are as follows:

- Making a unique or humorous outlook or comparison
- Taking a contrary point of view
- Creating questions that may include "what if" or "I wonder what"
- Find a piece of music, art, or a video clip to illustrate or define your annotation analysis
- Hypothesize about an author or speaker's motivation or intent

Making Connections

Brain Bits	Seek meaning, relevancy, and connections
Theaters of the Mind	Reflective Learning
Learning Styles	Microscope: visual learning
Research Basis	Questioning, cues and advanced organizers, homework
Grouping	Use with one, two, or three student groups.
Grade Level	This technique works for late elementary, middle level, and high school.
Timing	Use individually toward the end of the unit or for a formative assessment during the unit. Use as an assignment or for homework with two or three students at the beginning or middle of the unit.
Other Notes	Ask questions during group processing to support checking assumptions, author's point of view, and inferential thinking.

STEPS AND DIRECTIONS

Here are the four steps in the *iREAP* process:

1. *Read* to get the writer's basic message.

2. *Encode* the message into your own words while reading.

3. *Annotate* your analysis of the message by writing responses from several perspectives, including your own and at least one or two other students (a key strategy in building critical thinking).

4. *Ponder* what you have read and written; first by reviewing it yourself, then by sharing and discussing it with others, and finally by reading the responses of others.

The *i* before *REAP* is used when Internet sources or connections to others through technology are a part of the information used to gain perspectives.

■ SELECTED REFERENCES

Gregory and Kuzmich (2005b), Kuzmich (2007), Manzo, Manzo, and Albee (2002),

GRAPHIC ORGANIZER FOR: iREAP ■

Steps	To Do	Response
1. READ	What is the author's basic message? Use a phrase or two from the author.	
2. ENCODE	Put that main message into your own words in one or two complete sentences.	
3. ANNOTATE	Analyze this message from at least three points of view. Yours and two people involved in this assignment or text.	1. 2. 3.
4. PONDER	Read your response to others in the group or class and read their responses. How are the rest of the group members' responses the same or different from yours?	
5. INTERNET SOURCES	Cite your Internet source if that is what you used. Why is this piece of information an authentic source?	

◼ GRAPHIC ORGANIZER FOR: iREAP

Example for Grades 6–12

Name:

Class:

Source: *The Gettysburg Address*

Steps	To Do	Response
1. READ	What is the author's basic message? Use a phrase or two from the author.	"The brave men, living and dead, who struggled here have consecrated it far above our poor power to add or detract." "that this nation, under God, shall have a new birth of freedom . . ."
2. ENCODE	Put that main message into your own words in one or two complete sentences.	It is a dedication to the people that died fighting the Civil War and that we need to never forget the freedom they fought for and won for generations to follow.
3. ANNOTATE	Analyze this message from at least three points of view. Yours and two people involved in this assignment or text.	1. My View: This stirring address screams for us to remember what freedom is and how dear the price to preserve it. 2. Sharon's view: It is a call to unite and govern with the input of all people regardless of race. 3. Jose's view: It is about the horrors of war and that we should not forget those who died to give us or help us keep our freedom.
4. PONDER	Read your response to others in the group or class and read their responses. How are the rest of the group members' responses the same or different from yours?	We all have a slightly different viewpoint, mine is about freedom, Sharon's is about uniting all races, and Jose's is about remember those who sacrificed for this country. However, I think it is all about freedom and the price we pay to keep it. Lincoln is reminding us not to forget how important it is that we are united.
5. INTERNET SOURCES	Cite your Internet source if that is what you used. Why is this piece of information an authentic source?	We used the Library of Congress Web site. Since this is a government sponsored and well-known site it had the exact text we needed. We also listened to the address being read on Encarta online.

GRAPHIC ORGANIZER FOR: iREAP ▪

Example for Grades: 4–6

Name:

Grade/Room:

Source: *Goldilocks*

Steps	To Do	Response
1. READ	What is the author's basic message? Use a phrase or two from the author.	Who ate my porridge? That is just right!
2. ENCODE	Put that main message into your own words in one or two complete sentences.	You should get permission before using someone else's stuff.
3. ANNOTATE	Analyze this message from at least three points of view. Yours and two people involved in this assignment or text.	1. I think Goldilocks was dumb to go into someone else's house and use their stuff. 2. Tom said it was about being surprised by someone in your house. 3. Alicia said that Goldilocks was wrong to go into someone's house without permission.
4. PONDER	Read your response to others in the group or class and read their responses. How are the rest of the group members' responses the same or different from yours?	I think we all agreed that Goldilocks was wrong. We agreed that Alicia's idea about getting permission was important and different from the ideas Tom and I had thought about.
5. INTERNET SOURCES	Cite your Internet source if that is what you used. Why is this piece of information an authentic source?	http://www.surlalunefairytales.com/goldilocks/notes.html#TWENTY We used this Web site to read the story and understand the key phrases. The site has been around since 1998 and our librarian had it on a list of OK sites. This site is sponsored by Amazon.com.

INTEGRATING AND APPLYING LEARNING

Question Cubing

■ PURPOSE AND DESCRIPTION

This method helps student teams practice answering higher level questions and reviewing content work and creates opportunities for easy differentiation. Teachers may create different cubes related to a topic that provide different levels of readiness, offering an appropriate challenge without boring or stressing the learner. Cubes may also be related to Gardner's eight multiple intelligences:

Verbal-Linguistic	Interpersonal
Musical-Rhythmic	Intrapersonal
Visual-Spatial	Naturalistic
Bodily-Kinesthetic	Logical-Mathematical

These may appeal to the diverse learners' strengths, which can be used to process and comprehend new materials.

Making Connections

Brain Bits	This process emphasizes the brain's way of responding to challenges in a safe way, a way of establishing relationships between the known and unknown, provides needed collaboration and sharing to reach higher levels of thinking, make sense of information and respond to immediate feedback from peers and teacher.
Theaters of the Mind	Reflective and Cognitive Learning
Learning Styles	Beach Ball: creativity, Microscope: problem solving, Clipboard: process-based thinking, Puppy: processing, Interpersonal: random and sequential
Research Basis	Questioning, cues and advanced organizers, analysis, scaffolding thinking, metacognition strategies, foldables, testing hypotheses
Grouping	Use with groups of two to six students depending on desired thinking level. For comprehension cubing groups up to six work fine, for analysis, synthesis, and evaluation try groups of two and three so that all students get sufficient rehearsal and participation time with more complex thinking.
Grade Level	This technique works for late elementary, middle level, and high school. For younger or less-literate students this could be used as a whole-group discussion tool to model this type of thinking or use cubes with visuals instead of just words and a verbal question or prompt.

Timing	Provide 5 to 20 minutes depending on how many questions students tackle. Requires prior modeling by teacher or role playing by a couple of students used as models for discussion and feedback.
	Use at any point in the unit; if it is the beginning, select easier questions; if it is the end or middle of the unit, use more complex questions.
Other Notes	Prepare questions on cube or have students construct cubes and use a list of questions to pick from for their cube.
	Each team could answer one of the six questions and then combine this with jigsaw.
	Combine this with more than oral discussion for added critical thinking by having students write small group or individual responses or a combination of some shared and some individual written responses.
	Keep a basket of cubes available to increase the rigor at the closing of a lesson or as a bell or warm-up strategy to review previous work.
	Use as an assessment tool, select questions for different levels of learners to answer, or have students self-select to add a differentiation component. For assessment purposes, individual student responses will provide useful information about both content and the level of thinking about that content.

STEPS AND DIRECTIONS

1. Copy or prepare the outline of an unfolded cube

2. Add questions prior to duplication or have students add questions after duplication of a blank outline of a unfolded cube

3. Select topic and help students understand the prompt

4. Select grouping configuration and assign roles, like facilitator, questioner, recorder, summarizer, and so on. Using heterogeneous grouping helps make a larger group work even better and allows differentiation of roles to match difficulty level

5. Select a method of responding and sharing, oral, written, chart based, journal entry, quick write, and what the expectations are for quality

6. Model at least one or two acceptable responses

7. Circulate and give prompt feedback as students work

8. Plan to give feedback on thinking as well as content to students' oral or written responses

9. Create specific cubes for specific units or general cubes to use for all units

10. Save cubes for future use or give back with feedback if student created

SELECTED REFERENCES ■

Gregory and Chapman (2007), Gregory and Kuzmich (2005a, 2005b)

Ideas for Question Cubing:

■ SET ONE

1. **Describing:** Physically describe your topic. What does it look like? What color, shape, texture, size is it? Identify its parts.

2. **Comparing:** How is your topic similar to other topics and/or things? How is it different?

3. **Associating:** What other topic and/or thing does your topic make you think of? Can you compare it to anything else in your experience? Don't be afraid to be creative here: include everything that comes to mind.

4. **Analyzing:** Look at your topic's components. How are these parts related? How is it put together? Where did it come from? Where is it going?

5. **Applying:** What can you do with your topic? What uses does it have?

6. **Arguing:** What arguments can you make for or against your topic?

Source: Adapted from Axelrod, (1993), Meyer and Smith (1987).

■ SET TWO

1. **Describe it:** Look at the details.

2. **Compare it:** How is it the same as or different from? . . .

3. **Associate it:** Connect it with something.

4. **Analyze it:** Tell how it was made.

5. **Apply it:** What can you do with it?

6. **Argue for it or against it:** Use any approach or reasoning you want.

Source: Adapted from Gregory and Chapman, 2007, and the authors in the example above.

■ SET THREE: SELECT FROM THESE ANALYSIS STEMS FOR YOUR CUBE

Which events could have happened . . . ?

If . . . happened, what might the ending have been?

How was this similar to . . . ?

What was the underlying theme of . . . ?

What do you see as other possible outcomes?

Why did . . . changes occur?

Can you compare your . . . with that presented in . . . ?

Can you explain what must have happened when . . . ?

How is . . . similar to . . . ?

What are some of the problems of . . . ?

Can you distinguish between . . . ?

What were some of the motives behind . . . ?

What was the turning point in the game?

What was the problem with . . . ?

SET FOUR: SELECT FROM THESE ■ SYNTHESIS STEMS FOR YOUR CUBE

Can you design a . . . to . . . ?

Why not compose a song about . . . ?

Can you compose a poem about . . . ?

Can you see a possible solution to . . . ?

If you had access to all resources how would you deal with . . . ?

Why don't you devise your own way to deal with . . . ?

What would happen if . . . ?

How many ways can you . . . ?

Can you create new and unusual uses for . . . ?

Can you write a new . . . for . . . ?

How could you develop a proposal that would . . . ?

SET FIVE: SELECT FROM THESE ■ EVALUATION STEMS FOR YOUR CUBE

Is there a better solution to . . . ?

Judge the value of . . . .

Can you defend your position about . . . ?

Do you think . . . is a good or a bad thing?

How would you have handled . . . ?

What changes to . . . would you recommend?

Do you believe . . . about . . . ? Why?

Are you a . . . person?

How effective are . . . ?

What do you think about . . . ?

Why or why not?

Can you prove it?

More Words to Use to Form Higher Level Questions for Your Cubes

Set standards for evaluating the following:

— which are good, bad?

— which one(s) do you like?

— what do you think are the most likely?

— rate from good to poor

— select and choose

— is that good or bad?

— weigh according to the standards

— judge by how you feel

— what is the problem?

— are these solutions adequate?

— will it work?

— decide which

Source: Sets three to five and *More Words for Your Cubes* are adapted from: Bloom, (1980) and *All Our Children Learning*. New York: McGraw-Hill. Bloom, (1984). (see also http://www.teachers.ash.org.au/researchskills/dalton.htm)

■ ADAPTATIONS FOR PRIMARY GRADES

1. Create four cubes with pictures depicting each season on separate cubes. Have students talk about each picture and what season it belongs with; be certain to model answer the question: Why or why not?

2. Create cubes with patterns, numbers, or symbols that go together. Ask, "What is the rule for being included on this cube? Why are all of these things on this cube? What is the title of this cube?" and so on.

3. Create cubes with objects of a certain color (have students do it).

4. Create cubes with objects that start with a certain letter (have students do it).

5. Provide parts of anything like a plant, a meal, a house, a classroom, and then tell what it is and what each part is for, why it goes on the cube or fits with the others.

Thinking Cube

Describe It
Examine the subject closely and describe what you see.

Associate It
What does the subject make you think of? What does it remind you of?

Compare and Contrast
What is similar to it? What is different from it?

Analyze It
Break the subject into parts. Name the parts.

Argue For or Against It
Tell why you think it is good or not good.

Apply It
Tell how it is used.

SOURCE: Gregory and Chapman, 2007

INTEGRATING AND APPLYING LEARNING
Cause and Effect

■ PURPOSE AND DESCRIPTION

This method helps students practice the highest levels of analysis thinking, inference, and evaluation. Getting students to dig deeply into meaning and understanding of complex issues, problems, impacts of actions, and other factors for causal reasoning allows sufficient practice for anticipating future learning as well.

Making Connections

Brain Bits	This process emphasizes the impact of deeper thinking using collaborative learning and developing patterns and connections. Relevancy in relationship to an effect is an important element of developing cause-based thinking, one that is key to our survival and lifelong learning.
Theaters of the Mind	Reflective, Social, and Cognitive Learning
Learning Styles	Beach Ball: creativity, Microscope: problem solving, Clipboard: process-based thinking, Puppy: processing, Interpersonal: random and sequential
Research Basis	Questioning, cues and advanced organizers, analysis, scaffolding thinking, metacognition strategies, generating hypotheses, and summarizing
Grouping	Use with groups of two to three students or even individually for formative assessments. Cause-and-effect analysis requires dialogue and pairs talk more than larger groups; this impacts the quality of the thinking and the conclusions drawn from the discussion.
Grade Level	This technique works for late elementary, middle level, and high school. For younger or less-literate students, this could be used as a whole-group discussion tool to model this type of thinking or use templates with visuals instead of just words and a verbal question or prompt.
Timing	Provide 10 to 60 minutes, depending on how much information students need to find or look up. Be certain to model use of the templates. Use toward the end of a unit to further develop and elaborate thinking about complex issues, themes, questions, data results, research, and so on.
Other Notes	Prepare and walk through a model with students first. Make certain they understand the difference between causes and effects. English language learners and some students with learning disabilities may need a word bank, data source, or their notes to use while completing this process.

Assign roles by evens in the pair or triad, who writes, who reports out, who looks up information, and so on.

Try having pairs share with another pair and then refine their cause-and-effect organizer based on the wisdom of their peers prior to turning this in or reporting conclusions. This maximizes the impact of collaboration to deepen one's own thinking through sharing and oral discussion.

This works well on researched issues, science experiments or scientific information, mathematical strategic thinking, simple or complex social, political, economic issues, any cause-and-effect-based phenomena, even human behavior in works of fiction. Use with prose sources of information and nonprose documents such as charts, maps, tables, and Internet sites. Students can also collect data to prove or disprove speculative causes.

STEPS AND DIRECTIONS

1. Copy or prepare the template of your choice.

2. Model the thinking and check for understanding on the terms cause and effect.

3. Discuss with students the effect they are reviewing and analyzing; have students take notes or fill in that part of the organizer. With older students, especially high school, they can develop wording for the effect on their own, just be certain they do this first prior to working on the causes. Also, check for accuracy on their "effect statements." For students in fourth grade and up, the effect can be a hypothesis that is tested as well as a phenomenon that has already occurred. They can then discuss the accuracy of predicted causes. This takes more practice and rehearsal, but is well worth the effort to build deep analysis, synthesis, and evaluative thinking.

4. After examples of at least one possible cause, have students brainstorm possible causes. If you are using the fishbone, do this on another piece of paper and then have students organize the brainstorm list into categories, name the categories, and then transfer this to the fishbone. If you are using the Table Template, the brainstorm list can go right on the template. Be certain to prelabel the categories on the Table Template and then students can do this one by one.

5. Have students prepare an oral or written summary of their findings on the major causes for the effect.

SELECTED REFERENCES ■

Gregory and Kuzmich (2004), Gregory and Kuzmich (2005a, 2005b), Kuzmich (1999)

Fishbone

This organizer helps examine cause and effect or could be used for problem solving. The issue or problem is placed in the front box, and categories relating to the topic are place in the horizontal boxes. Attributes are added on the fish bones. This can also be used in any content area for note taking and summarizing. It may provide the "big picture" or advance organizer at the beginning of a unit of study with the headings in place and throughout the lessons students add pertinent information to the columns of the fishbone.

■ SECONDARY EXAMPLE: FISHBONE FOR IRAQ WAR

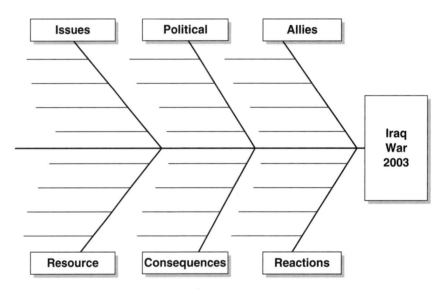

Summarize the most important ideas from your analysis in a short paragraph below:

ELEMENTARY OR MIDDLE SCHOOL EXAMPLE: ■
MELTING ICE AT THE POLAR REGIONS

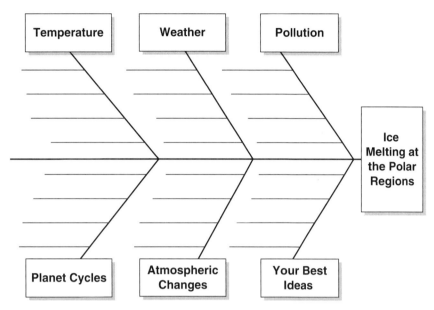

Summarize the most important ideas from your analysis in a short paragraph below:

■ **TEMPLATE FOR FISHBONE GRAPHIC**

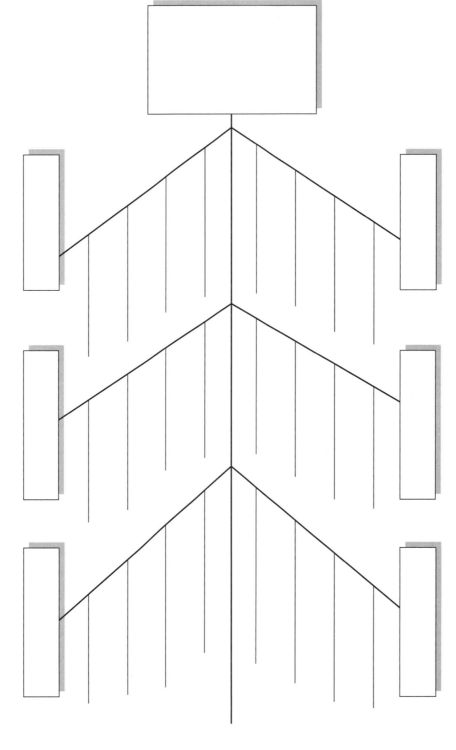

Summarize the most important ideas from your analysis in a short paragraph below:

TEMPLATE FOR TABLE CAUSE- AND-EFFECT ANALYSIS ▪

Effect: _____

_____

Teacher Note: To increase the rigor and relevance of this analysis, have students develop their own categories from research or do this as a class and come to agreement on at least four of the category titles, especially for secondary students. You can also add a predication piece of writing after the summary to increase and deepen thinking.

Cause Category and Details	Cause Category and Details
Cause Category and Details	Cause Category and Details
Cause Category and Details	Cause Category and Details

Summarize the most important ideas from your analysis in a short paragraph below:

Now, predict what would happen if . . . (variables or causes change):

■ ELEMENTARY EXAMPLE FOR TABLE CAUSE-AND-EFFECT ANALYSIS

Effect: Seasons Change

Directions: *Brainstorm your cause-based ideas and key information from your research on the table below.*

Movement of the Earth	The Sun
Where We Live on Earth	Weather Changes
Why We Need Seasons to Change	Your Other Great Thoughts on Causes

Summarize the most important ideas from your analysis in a short paragraph below:

SECONDARY EXAMPLE FOR TABLE ■
CAUSE-AND-EFFECT ANALYSIS

Effect: Economic Recession

Directions: *Brainstorm your cause-based ideas and key information from your research on the table below.*

Delivery of Goods and Services	Stock Market
Inflation, Deflation, Stagflation	Employment and Unemployment
Consumer Demand	Your Other Great Thoughts on Causes

Summarize the most important ideas from your analysis in a short paragraph below:

In another paragraph speculate on what it would take to end a recession once it begins:

INTEGRATING AND APPLYING LEARNING
Right Angle

■ PURPOSE AND DESCRIPTION

This is effective as a reflection tool for looking at a concept or issue and responding to it on both a factual and evaluative level. This deepens comprehension and is a great scaffolding method prior to creating a summary or analysis. Right Angle is a graphic organizer that works well with individual students and in small cooperative groups. It is also a great literacy tool, since a piece of text (fiction or nonfiction) or a nonprose source (charts, maps, Web sites, etc.) can be used for the facts. This tool helps students with inferential thinking as they pull the most important facts from a resource and then demonstrate their understanding of those facts as they offer or develop consensus around opinions, reactions, implications, and solutions about the concept or issue.

Making Connections

Brain Bits	Emotional impact and social support, development of cognitive learning in terms of developing common vocabulary, clarifying and sharing
Theaters of the Mind	Emotional, Cognitive, and Reflective Learning
Learning Styles	Microscope: analytical, Clipboard: organization
Research Basis	Questioning, cues and advanced organizers
Grouping	Use individually to respond to text or other sources or with groups of one to four students.
Grade Level Course	This technique works for all levels, elementary, middle level, and high school. Primary grades may need to use it as a shared writing or whole-group activity modeled by the teacher. Works well for controversial issues and analysis in secondary courses.
Timing	Use at the beginning or middle of a unit to further develop abstract concepts or central themes of a unit. Takes 10 to 30 minutes depending on the issue and resources used.
Other Notes	Set room up for partners or groups of four or fewer. Use template or large chart paper. May need text or other resources to get facts. Could also use survey or observations as sources of information for this strategy. May need to supply students with additional questions to assist with opinions, implications, reactions, or suggested solutions. Model the process as a whole class first. Right Angle works well for text and needs to be modified for Web sites, charts, maps and graphs, and other visual sources (see secondary example).

STEPS AND DIRECTIONS

1. Read or view a source of information about a difficult or central concept, an issue or topic in a unit.

2. Discuss and/or highlight the most important information in the text or visual material.

3. At the right-hand side of the right angle, one person fills in the facts related to the topic or issue.

4. Brainstorm opinions, reactions, implications, or solutions depending on the prompt or question being addressed by the student or learning team.

5. At the bottom, one responds to the issue with opinions, reactions, or feelings.

6. Optional directions for secondary students using technical or non-prose documents, technology, or mathematical resources: For non-prose visual materials complete the "fact-based purpose" of the Web site or document and then discuss the actions portion of the modified Right Angle.

SELECTED REFERENCES ■

Bellanca (1990), Burke (1993), Gregory and Kuzmich (2005a, 2005b), Gregory and Parry (2006), Junior Reserve Officers Training Corps (2006), Kuzmich (2007), Murphy (1994), North Central Regional Educational Laboratory (NCREL) (2006)

Facts

Right Angle

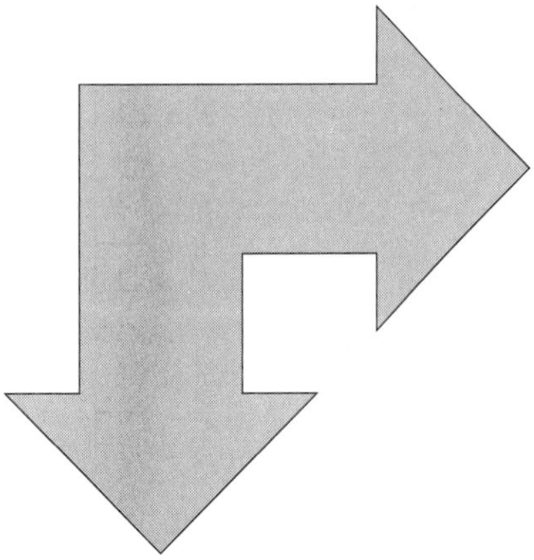

_____

_____

_____

_____

_____

_____

Opinions, Reactions, Implications

_____

_____

_____

_____

Right Angle

Subject: Science—The Environment

Grade: Primary Grades

Prompt: How can we help the environment stay healthy?

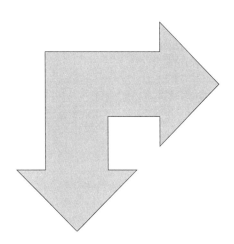

Facts:

1. We have lots of garbage on the school lawn.

2. Paper, cans, newspapers, and plastic bottles can be recycled or reused.

3. We don't put the right things in the recycle bins at lunch.

Opinions, Reactions, Implications

Our team came up with these ideas to help the environment at our school:

- Each week a different class could pick up the garbage on the school lawn.
- We could train all the kids at our school to put the right things in the right bins at lunch. Kids could stand by the bins to help the new students and the younger students.
- We could add a job in each class at our school. A student could help recycle and sort things for our bins each day and take them down to the gym.

RIGHT ANGLE ON ACTIONS:

Secondary Economics Example

Document or Source: Web site for comparing automobiles

Task: Convincing my parents to help me purchase an automobile after I graduate

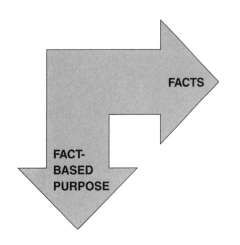

1. List Key Facts:

- Site updated 2006 (current)
- Contains searchable consumer information about multiple products (comprehensive, searchable)
- Has current links to other current sites (linkable)
- Allows comparisons between 3 to 4 products after customization
- Allows customization of options or features in a check box format (modifiable)
- Has pictures that change with options packages (enhanceable)
- I can e-mail the results to myself or my parents (collaborative)
- Has linkable loan information

2. What do you want to accomplish?

I need to find the best value for an automobile I can afford right after high school.

- I will be making less than $10/hr while attending school (about 30 hours a week)
- My parents are giving me $500 as a graduation gift
- My parents will co-sign on a 5-year loan or less
- I have to pay gas, my parents will help with $500 a year toward insurance

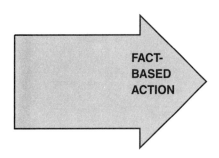

3. What actions will you take?

1. Review the information on economical cars including test results and repair costs.

2. Try out the Web site creating one economical car with the options I want, to test out the Web site.

3. Choose a few different scenarios to compare and e-mail myself the results.

4. Compare current loan results for the car I want.

5. Compare these results to a search for used cars.

6. Develop two or three possible scenarios to share with my parents including any charts or graphs of my wages, auto expenses, and other information. Plan to discuss this with my parents.

SOURCE: Reprinted with Permission: *Redefining Literacy for the 21st Century: Document, Technological, and Quantitative Literacy Strategies for Grades 7–12*. Kuzmich (2007). Rexford, NY: International Center for Leadership in Education.

INTEGRATING AND APPLYING LEARNING

Synectics

PURPOSE AND DESCRIPTION ■

The use of Synectics in the classroom leads students through a process that results in a three-dimensional view of the "problem" in order to create solutions. This process results in expanding student scope and depth of thinking. Uses research-based metaphor and simile thinking and helps students develop the fluidity and flexibility needed for creative solution design. Synectics (Gordon, 1961) provides an approach to creative thinking that depends on looking at what appears on the surface as unrelated phenomenon and drawing relevant connections. Synectics uses analogies or metaphors to improve cognitive flexibility and creativity. The approach, when used in cooperative groups, helps students develop creative responses to problem solving, to retain new information, to assist in generating writing, and to explore problems. It helps users expand existing minds sets, internalize abstract concepts, and increase long-term memory. Synectics also is a method of comparing and contrasting that is on the "best dressed" list of instructional practices and is a robust thinking skill. Anytime learners compare two ideas or concepts, they must be aware of the attributes of each to begin with and then take it to the next level of thinking by finding like and unlike characteristics.

Making Connections

Brain Bits	This process emphasizes the impact of deeper thinking using collaborative learning and developing patterns and connections. Creativity is a process that can be rehearsed and cultivated by developing cognitive flexibility and new connections to learning complex ideas, processes, or products.
Theaters of the Mind	Reflective, Social, and Cognitive Learning
Learning Styles	Beach Ball: creativity, Microscope: problem solving, Clipboard: process-based thinking, Puppy: processing, Interpersonal: random and sequential
Research Basis	Questioning, cues and advanced organizers, analysis, scaffolding thinking, metacognition strategies, generating metaphors and similes, synthesis, integration of learning, and creative responsiveness.
Grouping	Use with groups of two to three students or even individually for formative assessments. Synectics requires dialogue and pairs talk more than larger groups; this impacts the quality of the thinking and the conclusions drawn from the discussion.
Grade Level	This technique works for late elementary, middle level, and high school. For younger or less-literate students, this could be used as a whole-group discussion tool to model this type of thinking or use templates with visuals instead of just words and a verbal question or prompt.

Timing	Provide 10 to 60 minutes depending on how much information students need to find or look up. Be certain to model use of the templates.
	Use toward the middle of a unit to further develop and elaborate thinking about complex issues, themes, questions, data results, and research so that the summative assessment results in deeper thinking and creativity.
Other Notes	Prepare and walk through a model with students first. Make certain they understand the difference between metaphors and similes.
	English language learners and some students with learning disabilities may need a word bank, data source, or their notes to use while completing this process.
	Assign roles in the pair or triad—who writes, who reports out, who looks up information, and so on.
	See Four Squares for Creativity to practice the four aspects of creative thinking in addition to Synectics.
	This works well on abstract and complex concepts, developing creative solutions to problems, and inventing new ways to view things.

STEPS AND DIRECTIONS

1. Copy or prepare the template of your choice.

2. Model the use of Synectics in the classroom by leading students through a process that results in a three-dimensional view of the "problem" in order to create solutions. Although this process appears a bit cumbersome, the resultant scope and depth of your options will justify the time spent.

3. Create direct analogies: *What words have the same or similar meaning?* (Use a Thesaurus, word bank, book of synonyms, the Internet, or generate your own analogies.)

4. Describe personal analogies: *What would it feel like to have the characteristics or traits of . . . ?* (Describe emotions, implications of characteristics, and physical attributes.)

5. Identify compressed conflicts: *What words have the opposite meaning or characteristics?* (Use a book of antonyms, Thesaurus, word back, the Internet, or generate your own antonyms.)

6. Create a new direct analogy: *What words have the same or similar meaning?* (Use a source to help you that you did not use in Step 3 above.) Yes, this repeats the prompt from the second step. The difference, after going through the first three lists, you will have gone deeper into the subject, and this list will reflect that depth.

7. Synthesis: Look at all four lists and find key words or phrases; expand on those to generate more. Finally, focus on a theme that may incorporate several elements based on the final list.

8. Define the word(s): Put a definition in your own words to define each word, concept, or theme. Only after putting the definition in your own words can you compare your thoughts to those in a dictionary or glossary. Have students tell or write why their definition is better. Never copy a definition of a word; it causes regression in test scores and poor memory of the concept.

9. To ensure a fresh view, generate each of the following lists separately, put the current list away, and start the next list after a break of at least 5 to 10 minutes. If time permits, longer breaks yield more beneficial results.

   Note: When using Synectics to define a person appropriate for self-evaluation, focus your questions on the areas of physical attributes, skills, interests, personality traits, attitudes, and emotional states.

10. Have students prepare an oral or written definition to share, or create this chart on large paper for the whole class to see, or even use PowerPoint for group sharing.

SELECTED REFERENCES ■

Gordon (1961), Prince (1970), Roukes (1988)

■ **TEMPLATE FOR SYNECTICS**

Concept, Theme, or Phenomena				
Similar	*Feels Like*	*Opposite*	*Similar and/or Additional Sources*	*Synthesis*

Definition in Your Own Words:

Other Possible Prompts to Extend the Learning and Thinking Further:

1. How did you change your mind about the original issue after completing this process?

2. How would people in other parts of the world have defined this idea, theme, or explained the phenomena?

3. How would you teach someone else what you have learned?

POSSIBLE SECONDARY TOPICS ■
TO USE WITH SYNECTICS

advertising	fidelity	justice	restraint
affirmative action	films	libelous	restriction
anarchy	fashionable	nationalism	righteousness
anti-Semitism	freedom	naturalism	sabotage
appropriateness	gender equity	nonpartisanship	security
bias	genocide	objectionable	secularism
bigotry	glass ceiling	obscenity	sexual harassment
books	harmony	offensive	slander
cable television	heroism	partisanship	society
chaos	heterogeneous	peace	Spanish Inquisition
chauvinism	imagination	personal diaries	standards
civilization	inflammatory	politically correct	stocks
computer hackers	institutional racism	pornography	submission
communism	interference	prejudice	suppression
conformity	Internet	privacy	television
conservative	intimidation	prohibited	theft
crime	intolerance	propaganda	threat
democracy	invasion	protectionism	tolerance
discrimination	investigation	racism	unclean
disruption	liberty	radio	Victorianism
domination	liberalism	reasonable	video
e-mail	magazines	religion	violation
education	mail fraud	religious right	violence
espionage	morality	respect	war
exploitation	movies	repression	warranties
exploration	murder	responsible	
expression			
evolution			

We could all add to this list from any content area. You can also add people's names, government functions and agencies, math strategies, variable qualities and types, organizations, specific music, specific behaviors, and so on. Any controversial, difficult, or abstract concept works very well with Synectics.

■ ELEMENTARY ADAPTATION OF THE MODEL

Elementary Templates for Synectics

Concept, Theme, or Phenomena				
Similar	*Feels Like*	*Opposite*	*Importance*	*Part of What Else*

Definition in Your Own Words:

Teacher note for elementary version: Notice that the last two steps for elementary need to change to make this model less complex. It is highly recommended that this is a shared-writing experience with the whole class or small group to model the thinking. Perhaps provide students with word banks to pick from for the columns. Use this adjusted template with Grades 4 through 6.

For primary grade students, use this simple method and use with pictures or visuals before trying it with words.

1. This	2. Is to this
3. As this	4. Is to that

Primary Examples

1. This: fish	2. Is to this: water
3. As this: bird	4. Is to that: tree

Follow-Up Primary Questions:

1. Why is this true?

2. What else do we know about . . . ?

3. What else could be true?

4. Why is this important?

5. How does this relate to you?

6. What other ones can you think of to try this out?

Visual and word metaphors are powerful memory tools and help students get ready for more complex Synectics thinking.

Possible Elementary Topics to Use With Synectics

Any type of food Any type of person Any career Any place Most common nouns	Any type of system in science or social studies Any story element Any math concept	Any character traits Any behaviors Any attributes or actions of people or animals	Any parts to whole relationships Any big topics to little topics Any elements of a larger thing

5

Conclusion

Putting It All Together

We can impact student results and achievement growth when we pay attention to how the brain learns best. The research around best practices that align themselves with how the brain works are among the highest payoff activities we can use. These strategies engage learners. Without engagement learning does not occur. Every brain is unique, and as such, teachers need a multiplicity of strategies and techniques so all learners' brains are safe and engaged—thus, opening as many "theaters of the mind" as possible will reach diverse learners and differentiate points of entry and intrigue all students.

THEATERS OF THE MIND ▪

Taking one more look at Barbara Given's (2002a, 2002b) Theaters of the Mind helps us confirm the use of the strategies in this book and success for students. Differentiation is not a set of strategies but of more student-centered response to the range of students' readiness, learning profiles, and interests. Each theater needs to be "open" as often as possible to create a safe, engaging environment and a variety of ways to make sense of content and practice needed skills.

Social and Emotional Learning Systems

Most of the strategies such as *Find Someone Who* and *Random Partners* are socially satisfying. They allow the learner to share and validate personal ideas as well as gain perspective and additional points of view in an intimate non-threatening atmosphere. Students are much more likely to share their perspective and personal thoughts to another student rather than a whole class. Often sharing, even if the ideas are convoluted, can clarify their own thinking or modify it from a partner's perspective.

Physical Learning System

Interaction, movement, creation, hands-on materials with projects, models, and other materials satisfy the learner's need to get deeply involved, not just mentally but physically. Such physical interactions increase long-term memory and allow multiple pathways for concepts, making accessing background knowledge much easier. Many of the strategies in this book help learners with diverse styles and capabilities.

Cognitive Learning System

These strategies help students deepen understanding, apply and integrate content knowledge and skills. Students need rehearsal in different forms to increase memory. We tend to retrieve information more easily when we have multiple interactive experiences. All content is abstract, similar to a foreign language. We unpack abstract content when we have concrete experiences, symbolic representations, and are able to form our own meaning or definition. These strategies help us fill our need to rehearse content in multiple ways in short-term memory in order to move it to longer-term memory that helps us make connections and establish the ability to apply what we know.

Reflective Learning System

Students learn when we have their attention, when learners care about or are motivated by the work, and when students engage with each other. One of the best studies reviewing the research on cooperative learning was done by McVee, Dunsmore, and Gavelek in 2005. When content is viewed from multiple perspectives in small groups, students tend to remember the pertinent materials, are able to recall it, and are able to form new and deeper connections. Work in small groups coupled with great prompts, graphic organizers, and other strategies like the ones in this book help students deepen thinking.

THOUGHTFUL GROUPING OF STUDENTS   ■

Differentiation depends on the ability of teachers to facilitate cooperative group learning situations and the students' ability to work together successfully toward learning goals. In a differentiated classroom, students need to feel "brain safe" enough to be able to work with any partner or small group. Teachers need to teach social skills such as "active listening" to students so that they can interact optimally and be successful at learning and practicing knowledge and skills.

Teachers need to avoid giving students a sense of being a "bluebird" or a "buzzard" when creating grouping and collaboration opportunities. The key to successful differentiation is "flexible grouping" as required based on readiness, interest and strengths, or student needs. Heterogeneous grouping works far better to close gaps and get results, especially when students are learning from each other. Flexible grouping to teach a discrete skill when students need enrichment or reteaching is appropriate since this organization of students is a temporary response to data collection for learning proficiency. Homogeneous grouping works only for this purpose when the teacher is leading the flexible or temporary group. Our strategies are about engaging students, sharing skills for rehearsal and memory, and applying what we learned. These purposes lend themselves to heterogeneous grouping in terms of skill, literacy, and perhaps even behavior proficiency. James and Chen-Lin Kulik published a study in 1987 examining the effect of ability groupings on achievement, even among gifted learners. The study showed that students gained more in terms of achievement when grouped or teamed with students of varying ability. We highly recommend conversation and dialogue in every classroom, every day. The chart below helps remind teachers of some of the purposes and activities for different-size groupings.

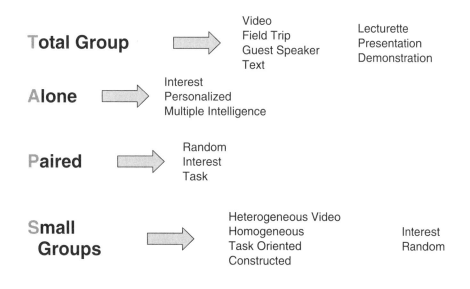

SOURCE: Gregory and Chapman (2007)

The greater the level of critical thinking, the smaller the group size should be since each student will need individual rehearsal. One easy rule to think about is that knowledge and comprehension can be delivered in whole or small groups, application is best in small groups of six or fewer, and analysis, synthesis, and evaluation is best delivered in small groups of three, pairs, or individual practice. Also, combinations of these groupings work well, and the critical-thinking demands change during a lesson or unit.

■ THE POWER OF USING GRAPHIC ORGANIZERS

The 29 major studies to date on the use and effectiveness of graphic organizers show us the profound impact we can have on instruction and assessment results. The effect sizes in these studies range from 0.5 to 0.91 in terms of increasing the probability of student success on assessments when these strategies are used frequently. Additional studies on the use of visual or nonlinguistic representations further confirm the impact of such methods. When we consider differentiation, we are aware that students have different visual, auditory, tactile, and/or kinesthetic preferences and needs in the learning process. Using a graphic organizer (visual) and working with a partner (auditory—both voices) and writing or drawing (tactile) satisfies multiple learners. If you have them moving around the room to retrieve supplies and or "scouting" (checking out other students' ideas), the kinesthetic learners also get their needs met.

Here is a list of the potential benefits of using graphic organizers from two of the major studies (Ausubel, 1963; Kim, Vaughn, Wanzek, & Wei, 2004).

Students will learn to do the following:

- Brainstorm ideas
- Develop, organize, and communicate ideas
- See connections, patterns, and relationships
- Share prior knowledge
- Develop vocabulary
- Outline for writing process activities
- Highlight important ideas
- Classify or categorize concepts, ideas, and information
- Comprehend the events in a story or book
- Improve social interaction between students and facilitate group work and collaboration among peers
- Guide review and study
- Deepen critical thinking
- Improve analysis, synthesis, and evaluation with appropriate prompts
- Improve reading comprehension skills and strategies
- Facilitate recall and retention

Teachers may also use organizers as formative assessments of content, vocabulary, comprehension, analysis, and other key factors for insuring that learning sticks.

Today's students have a natural affinity for visual material since their world continually surrounds them with rich visual input. There are many types of graphic organizers that are a type of nonlinguistic representation. These go by several different names. We shared some graphic organizers with you in this book that work well in combination with the power of dialogue and collaboration. Any graphic organizer can be turned into a dialogue opportunity for students. In a differentiated classroom, providing visual and verbal opportunities such as writing and speaking and recording on a graphic organizer also taps into both hemispheres of the brain and creates a double rehearsal (Buzan & Buzan 1994)—thus supporting those learners with a dominance in one hemisphere while also being more whole-brain oriented.

All Different Kinds

```
        Advanced              Thinking
       Organizers              Maps

   Mind Maps                          Foldables


                    Graphic
                   Organizers

   Concept                             Note
   Maps or                            Takers
   Diagrams


       Vocabulary                     Story
        Graphic                       Maps
       Organizers
                    Cognitive
                      Maps
```

SOURCE: Kuzmich (2008)

NOTE: Thinking Maps (thinkingmaps.com) and Foldables are both copyrighted materials; see Zike (1992).

There are all types of Web sites and books devoted to the topic. When we combine strategies with high effect sizes like cooperative group strategies with dialogue and collaboration and graphic organizers and visual representations, we increase the probability of student learning and success. These strategies are easy to differentiate when the prompt associated with group-based use of graphic organizers are open-ended. In addition, there are many examples in this book of open-ended prompts at higher levels of critical thinking. Graphic organizers also get students writing. Writing frequently increases thinking fluency. The impact of writing on achievement is well documented (Vantage Learning, 2007). When teachers are busy and they want to know which of the many strategies to select, we highly recommend a focus on these two research-based methods. Since students using graphic organizers significantly outperformed their peers, why not use this powerful strategy at least three or more times during the course of any unit of study over one or more weeks?

■ THE ROLE OF DIALOGUE IN LEARNING

Our brains are hardwired to learn from speaking and listening not reading and writing. However, if students have strong verbal skills and language patterns, reading and writing seem to flow. You do not learn language only by listening; you also have to use it. It is a biological necessity in effective learning and memory formation. Numerous studies show the benefit of student dialogue to deepen understanding, practice the language of academics, and draw from the experiences and perspectives of others. Feldman, Kinsella, and Stump (2002) pose a great question for teachers, "Have I prepared *all* of my students for the linguistic demands of this task?" (p. 1). If the teacher was the only one talking in class or just a few students responded to questions asked by the teacher, the answer is no. Student dialogue is an essential piece to academic success. David Conley's (2007) research on student readiness for college and post-secondary training indicates a high need for group learning. Students who can form study teams are much more likely to succeed in post-secondary education. However, students don't automatically know how to do this. The strategies in this book give students the rehearsal they need to become comfortable and competent in different-size groups all engaged in academic dialogue and group productivity. As teachers, we need to provide frequent and structured opportunities for student-academic dialogue. Today's Think-Pair-Share or Jigsaw might make a huge difference in the options and opportunities that students have after they leave us. Think-Pair-Share also provides an easy, low-preparation formative assessment for the teacher as she and/or he eavesdrops on the conversations and picks up information about which students "got it" and which are still needing clarification or further rehearsal. This is helpful for further differentiating the next steps for students.

EVALUATING AND GIVING FEEDBACK ON TEAMING SUCCESS ■

Student self-evaluation of his or her own performance in a group and that of the group itself is critical to the success of student teaming and a factor in the effect-size impact on cooperative learning in general. Following are some examples for group and self-evaluation. These rubrics and checklists should help both teachers and students reflect on the learning and the learning process using the research-based strategies in this book.

Please note that an additional column has been added, and students could do a self-reflection on their teaming skills as well as the teacher.

■ **ATTRIBUTES OF SUCCESSFUL TEAMS**

Skills Criteria 1 = None of the time 2 = Some of the time 3 = Most of the time 4 = All of the time	Team Rating	Teacher Rating
Helping Observed the students offering assistance to each other.		
Listening Observed students working from each other's ideas.		
Participating Observed each student contributing his or her portion to the project.		
Persuading Observed the students exchanging, defending, and rethinking ideas.		
Questioning Observed the students interacting, discussing, and posing questions to all members of the team.		
Respecting Observed the students encouraging and supporting the ideas and efforts of others.		
Sharing Observed the students offering ideas and reporting their findings to each other.		

Total Points from the Teacher: _____ Total Points from the Students: _____

Teacher Comments:

Student Comments:

SOURCE: Adapted in part from Hodgson and Vogelphol (2008); Gregory and Kuzmich (2007)

TEAMING-PURPOSE CHECKLISTS   ▪

Here are two forms of Teaming-Purpose Checklists from each section of this book for teachers to check for the desired results of teaming. You can rate the success of purposes as shown in the first version or use this as a teaching tool and communication system in the second example. You can give students feedback on the purpose for teaming. Students can self-evaluate using the checklists. You can also begin a teaming session by checking the key purposes for the teamwork today so that students know the intended results of their teaming efforts. Using checklists is a quick way of self-assessing that also provides formative assessment for teachers so that flexible groupings may be formed in the differentiated classroom based on current status.

Teaming-Purpose Checklist Format One:

Rate each of the following desired results of teaming as follows:

Plus or 3 if this is happening consistently as applicable

Check or 2 if this is happening periodically as applicable

Question mark or 1 if this is not observed or inconsistent

Teaming to Learn	Sharing Knowledge and Skills
____ Learning routines	____ Learning content
____ Understanding roles	____ Developing understanding
____ Developing team	____ Developing learning strategies
____ Celebrating success	____ Developing schema
____ Getting and giving feedback	____ Learning multiple routines
____ Communicating	____ Transferring
____ Building trust	____ Expanding options
____ Peer coaching	____ Sharing
____ Team process evaluation	____ Peer support
Integrating and Applying Learning	**Other Notes on Teaming Success:**
____ Learning to use knowledge	
____ Goal setting	
____ Increasing long-term memory	
____ Developing generalization	
____ Generating hypotheses	
____ Critical-thinking skills	
____ Analysis skills	
____ Problem-solving strategies	
____ Developing creativity	
____ Keeping teamwork successful	

Teaming-Purpose Checklist Format Two:

This form of the Teaming-Purpose Checklist can be duplicated on card stock or half sheets of paper for ease of use with students. This chart can be a poster size for older students. Then use the chart to teach the purpose for an upcoming teaming activity, to remind students what to demonstrate during teaming, and as a feedback tool. This can also be duplicated and cut into bookmark-size cards to distribute to teams as a reminder of what you are looking for as they work.

Teaming to Learn	Sharing Knowledge and Skills	Integrating and Applying Learning
• Learning routines	• Learning content	• Learning to use knowledge
• Understanding roles	• Developing understanding	• Goal setting
• Developing team	• Developing learning strategies	• Increasing long-term memory
• Celebrating success	• Developing schema	• Developing generalization
• Getting and giving feedback	• Learning multiple routines	• Generating hypotheses
• Communicating	• Transferring	• Critical-thinking skills
• Building trust	• Expanding options	• Analysis skills
• Peer coaching	• Sharing	• Problem-solving strategies
• Team process evaluation	• Peer support	• Developing creativity
		• Keeping teamwork successful

SELF-EVALUATION REPORTING FOR GREAT TEAM CONTRIBUTIONS ▪

Students write responses to these questions or share oral evaluation with team members. Team members can also practice giving each other positive feedback and suggestions for teaming. Rehearsal is necessary to keep this a learning experience.

1. Did I contribute my full share of work to the group? Why or why not? What other help do you need to get better at this?

2. Did I use my time with the group to help with their success and keep the group focused to finish our task? Why or why not? What other help do you need to get better at this?

3. Did you communicate with others to get everyone's needs met, clarify and assist with the learning task, and get a successful result from your work? Why or why not? What other help do you need to get better at this?

4. Other observations or comments about my contribution to our team.

■ TEACHER SELF-EVALUATION OF BUILDING TEAMS FOR SUCCESSFUL RESULTS

Give yourself a plus for each building block you felt resulted in student success, a check for results that might be emerging or inconsistent as yet, and an *R* for those you may need to reteach differently.

Rating: *Plus,* *Check, or* *R = Reteach*	*Building Blocks of Successful Teams*
	Building a knowledge of each other, each other's styles, and an appreciation of the diversity that makes teams better performing
	Developing respectful social skills and good communication to coordinate efforts
	Developing common understanding of learning tasks and criteria for learning success
	Developing the ability to picture successful teaming and each student's contribution to that success
	Setting group and individual goals for contributing to the teaming process and success
	Establishing a means of gathering and sharing resources
	Establishing rituals for feedback and celebration
	Analyzing how effectively the team worked together and getting students to accurately self-evaluate the team's performance

SELF-RATING FOR YOUNGER STUDENTS   ■

I think we did . . .	Teaming for Success	My teacher thinks we did . . .
Great	• We took turns. • We listened. • We asked good questions. • We did our work well.	**Great**
OK	• Not everyone had a turn. • We talked about the work. • We did our work OK.	**OK**
Not Yet	• We did not always get along. • We talked about other things. • We needed help to finish our work.	**Not Yet**

■ STRUGGLING LEARNERS

Learners struggle when messages and experiences of failure become too frequent. The damage can be prevented with early intervention. But is that not enough for some students? What about new immigrants or those learning English as another language? What about students with more severe disabilities? What about those who come from poverty? What about learners who need motivation to engage? What about those so bright they need challenging and advanced opportunities? What about learners who struggle to feel safe and to have sense of belonging? Our teachers in this country work in one of the best education systems in the world because we educate everyone. Very few countries have this intensive commitment. We would have it no other way. However, teachers need the support, resources, and skills to deal with the wide diversity we cherish as the cornerstone of our rights and responsibilities. Instead of writing about what different groups of students struggle with, let us take a look at what all students need regardless of success or failure. First, here is a basic toolkit of strategies that all teachers need; many more could be added:

The Basic Strategies in Accelerating Growth for All Learners:

❑ Asking questions (teacher and students)

❑ Avoiding assumptions

❑ Asking for help from specialist provides variety

❑ Providing no-fault practice and rehearsal

❑ Designing for variety over short periods of time

❑ Making connections and establishing purpose

❑ Increasing vocabulary through concept-based learning

❑ Creating opportunities to integrate complex ideas

❑ Creating a respectful climate for learning

❑ Providing and requiring modeling and self-evaluation

❑ Use grouping size and composition to increase thinking levels

❑ Checking for errors and detecting errors

❑ Organizing learning

❑ Using great literacy strategies

❑ Accessing learning through multiple modalities, styles, or intelligences

❑ Pre-assessment and formative assessment to make changes along the way

❑ Student goal setting, adjustment of goals, and evaluation of results

---

SOURCE: Gregory and Kuzmich (2005a)

In addition to great strategies, teachers must foster the relationships and engagement without which learning will not occur, especially in the differentiated classroom where flexible groups are evolving and students are working with everyone over the course of the week, and assignments and learning experiences may vary.

All students need the following basic human needs:

- Sense of belonging
- Sense of competence and worth
- Sense of safety
- Sense of individual and not just group identity
- Sense of accomplishment and goal reaching
- Sense of love and regard
- Sense of excitement about learning

All students deserve engaging and relevant instruction that builds critical thinking and the capacity for lifelong learning.

We are certain you could add to this list as well. What if we picked strategies that meet many of these needs and the needs of most subgroups we typically identify? Given the research and the impact on student well-being and achievement, we would argue for student teaming with wonderful opportunities for dialogue and collaboration and the use of visual representations and graphic organizers.

PLANNING FOR STUDENT TEAMS ■

Use these strategies alone or in combination. See the charts that follow for more guidance. Feel free to use the template and examples that come with this book. Also, please feel free to modify them for your particular grade level or content area.

Teaming to Learn	*Sharing Knowledge And Skills*	*Integrating and Applying Learning*
Purpose:	Purpose:	Purpose:
Learning routines	Learning content	Learning to use knowledge
Understanding roles	Developing understanding	Goal setting
Developing team	Developing learning strategies	Long-term memory
Celebrating success	Developing schema	Developing generalization
Getting and giving feedback	Learning multiple routines	Generating hypotheses
Communicating	Transferring	Critical-thinking skills
Building trust	Expanding options	Analysis skills
Peer coaching	Sharing	Problem-solving strategies
Team process evaluation	Peer support	Developing creativity
		Successful teamwork
1. Community Circle	8. ABC Conversations	15. Four Squares for Creativity
2. Find Someone Who	9. 3-2-1 with Consulting Line or Inside-Outside Circles	16. Point of View
3. Four-Corner Processing	10. Jigsaw Methods	17. iREAP
4. Random Partners	11. Concept Formation	18. Question Cubing
5. T-Chart and Y-Chart	12. Content Dialogue	19. Cause and Effect
6. Graffiti	13. Note Taking and Summarizing	20. Right Angle
7. Think-Pair-Share and Say and Switch	14. Wallpaper Poster	21. Synectics

Here is a way to plan for the use of strategies in this book and get your student teams going and achieving.

Instructional Purpose	Teaming to Learn	Sharing Knowledge and Skills	Integrating and Applying Learning
Getting teams started	X		
Reviewing learning before a test	X	X	X
Analysis, synthesis, and evaluation		X	X
Application and comprehension		X	X
Formative assessment	X	X	X
Feedback and praise	X	X	X
Deepening comprehension		X	X
Problem solving			X
Designing			X
Transfer of learning between classes or content		X	X
Reteaching	X	X	
Behavior or class management	X	X	
Summative assessment			X

Here is one more chart to help you think about the strategies from a different perspective. Many of the strategies we list work well for other aspects of learning with minor adjustments in the prompt or questions to get student teams going.

Strategy	Teaming to Learn	Sharing Knowledge and Skills	Integrating and Applying Learning
1. Community Circle	X	X	
2. Find Someone Who	X	X	
3. Four-Corner Processing	X	X	X
4. Random Partners	X	X	
5. T-Chart and Y-Chart	X	X	X
6. Graffiti	X	X	X
7. Think-Pair-Share and Say and Switch	X X	X X	X
8. ABC Conversations	X	X	X
9. Inside-Outside Circles	X	X	
10. Jigsaw Methods	X	X	X
11. Concept Formation	X	X	
12. Content Dialogue		X	X
13. Note Taking and Summarizing	X	X X	X
14. Wallpaper Poster	X	X	
15. Four Squares for Creativity		X	X
16. Point of View	X	X	X
17. iREAP	X	X	X
18. Cubing	X	X	X
19. Cause and Effect		X	X
20. Right Angle		X	X
21. Synectics		X	X

Take Cubing as an example; we list it under *Integrating and Applying Learning* because it is a perfect opportunity to deepen the thinking level of students about the content or skills; it can also be used when forming teams or sharing Knowledge and Skills.

We could change the questions on the cube to social or getting to know you questions like the following:

- What is your favorite computer or TV program?
- How did you get your name?
- What is your favorite way of learning?
- Do you like fiction or real-world material to read?
- What traits do you need in a friend?
- What helps you most as a member of a working team or group?

For sharing Knowledge and Skills we could ask these questions on our cube:

- What was the most important thing we need to remember about . . . ?
- What are the three vocabulary words that help us with this material, and what do they mean?
- What are the uses of . . . ?
- How could you describe that process to a new student?
- Why do you think that happened?
- What text message would you send to summarize this learning? Now translate for your grandmother.

FINAL THOUGHTS ■

In conclusion, an effective approach to building and sustaining student teams that focuses on results for each student helps promote an atmosphere of inquiry and rigor throughout the learning. We hope that your groups of students become high performance teams that get amazing results. Please take time to celebrate your successes and build off your accomplishments when it comes to student success.

Educators are heroic in their efforts to integrate emotion, relationship, and human interaction to influence learning. Hargreaves (1997) wrote,

> If our attempts to go wider in our change efforts are to be educationally productive . . . we must also go deeper and examine the moral grounds and emotional texture of our practice, of what it means to be a teacher. (p. 14)

We thank you for your "heroic" efforts and hope that as you deepen your thinking working with students, you get the results you seek for your children and for their future. We think that high-yield strategies like the ones we offer here improve the probability that all of your students will make progress and reach the targets you have set for learning and growth. We hope these tools help you become an educator that gets results. We salute your efforts and your desire to increase growth and achievement for students since this will impact the future our students will create!

References

Aronson, E., Blaney, N., Stephin, C., Sikes, J., & Snapp, M. (1978). *The jigsaw classroom*. Beverly Hills, CA: Sage.

Australian Government Department of Education. (2006). *My read.* Retrieved August 28, 2006, from http://www.myread.org/index.htm

Ausubel, D. (1963). *The psychology of meaningful verbal learning*. New York: Grune & Stratton.

Axelrod, R. B., & Cooper, C. R. (1993). *The Concise Guide to Writing*. New York: St. Martin's.

Barell, J. (2003). *Developing more curious minds*. Alexandria, VA: ASCD.

Beaudoin, M., & Taylor, M. (2004). *Creating a positive school culture: How principals and teachers can solve problems together*. Thousand Oaks, CA: Corwin.

Bellanca, J. (1990). *The cooperative think tank*. Thousand Oaks, CA: Corwin.

Bellanca, J., & Fogarty, R. (1994). *Blueprints for thinking in the cooperative classroom*. Heatherton, Australia: Hawker Brownlow Education.

Bennett, B., & Rolheiser, C. (2001). *Beyond Monet*. Toronto, Canada: Bookation.

Bennett, B., Rolheiser, C., & Stevahn, L. (1991). *Cooperative learning: Where heart meets mind*. Toronto, Canada: Educational Connections.

Bloom, B. S. (1980). *All our children learning*. New York: McGraw-Hill.

Bloom, B. S. (1984). *Taxonomy of educational objectives*. Boston: Allyn & Bacon.

Brock, F. (1986). The effects of referential questions on ESL classroom discourse. TESOL Quarterly, *20*, 47–59.

Brown, J., & Moffat, C. (1999). *The hero's journey: How educators can transform schools and improve learning*. Alexandria, VA: ASCD.

Buehl, D. (1995). *Classroom strategies for interactive learning*. Randolf, WI: Wisconsin State Reading Association.

Buehl, D. (2006). *Hearing "voices" as you read*. Retrieved August 28, 2006, from http://wilearns.state.wi.us/apps/default.asp?cid=718

Burke, K. (1993). *The mindful school: How to assess thoughtful outcomes*. Palatine, IL: IRI/Skylight.

Buzan, T., & Buzan, B. (1994). *The mind map book*. New York: NAL-Dutton.

Chadwick, B. (2006). *"The circle" and "grounding."* Retrieved April 2006, from http://www.managingwholes.com/power.htm

Chang R., & Buster, S. (1999). *Step-by-step problem solving in education*. Houston, TX APQC

Chang, R., & Dalziel, D. (1999a). *Continuous improvement tools in education, Vol. 1*. Houston, TX: APQC.

Chang, R., & Dalziel, D. (1999b). *Continuous improvement tools in education, Vol. 2*. Houston, TX: APQC.

Conley, D. (2007, March). *Redefining college readiness.* Eugene, OR: Educational Policy Improvement Center.

Costa, A., & Garmston, R. (2002). *Cognitive coaching: A foundation for renaissance schools* (2nd ed.). Norwood, MA: Christopher-Gordon.

Dalton, J., & Smith, D. (1986). *Extending children's special abilities—Strategies for primary classrooms.* Retrieved September 5, 2009, from http://www.teachers.ash.org.au/researchskills/dalton.htm

Daniels, W. (1986). *Group power I: A manager's guide to using task force meetings.* San Diego, CA: University Associates, and Johnson & Johnson.

Deal, T., & Peterson, K. (1998). *Shaping school culture: the heart of leadership.* San Francisco: Jossey-bass.

Elder, L., & Paul, R. (2002). *Instructor's manual for critical thinking tools for taking charge of your learning and your life.* San Francisco: Foundation for Critical Thinking.

Erickson, L. (2005). *Concept based curriculum and instruction.* Thousand Oaks, CA: Corwin.

Feldman, K., Kinsella, K., & Stump, C. (2002). *Language strategies for active* classroom *participation.* Needham Heights, MA: Allyn & Bacon.

Garmston, R. (1996). Triple track presenting. *Journal of Staff Development, 17*(2). Retrieved June 2, 2009, from http://www.nsdc.org/news/jsd/garmston172.cfm

Gibbs, J. (2001). *Tribes: A new way of learning and being together.* Windsor, CA: Center Source Systems, LLC.

Given, B. K. (2002a). *The brain's natural learning systems.* Alexandria, VA: ASCD.

Given, B. K. (2002b). *Teaching to the brain's natural learning systems.* Alexandria VA: ASCD.

Goleman, D. (1995). *Emotional intelligence.* New York: Bantam.

Gordon, W. (1961). *Synectics.* New York: Harper and Row.

Gregory, G. (2006). *Differentiating instruction with style.* Thousand Oaks, CA: Corwin.

Gregory, G., & Chapman, C. (2007). *Differentiated instructional strategies: One size doesn't fit all* (2nd ed.). Thousand Oaks, CA: Corwin.

Gregory, G., & Kuzmich, L. (2004). *Data-driven differentiation in the standards-based classroom.* Thousand Oaks, CA: Corwin.

Gregory, G., & Kuzmich, L. (2005a). *Differentiated literacy strategies for student growth and achievement grades K–6.* Thousand Oaks, CA: Corwin.

Gregory, G., & Kuzmich, L. (2005b). *Differentiated literacy strategies for student growth and achievement grades 7–12.* Thousand Oaks, CA: Corwin.

Gregory, G., & Kuzmich, L. (2007). *Teacher teams that get results.* Thousand Oaks, CA: Corwin.

Gregory, G., & Parry, T. (2006). *Designing brain compatible learning.* Thousand Oaks, CA: Corwin.

Gregory, G., Robbins, P., & Herndon, L. (2000). *Teaching inside the block schedule: Strategies for teaching in extended periods of time.* Thousand Oaks, CA: Corwin.

Gruenfeld, D., & Hollingshead, A. (1993). Sociocognition in work groups: The evolution of group integrative complexity and its relation to task performance. Research done at the University of Illinois at Urbana-Champaign in *Small Group Research, 24*(3), 383–405.

Hargreaves, A. (1997). Rethinking educational change. In A. Hargreaves (Ed.), *Rethinking educational change with heart and mind: 1997 ASCD yearbook* (pp. 14–33). Alexandria, VA: ASCD.

Harmin, M. (1995). *Strategies to inspire active learning.* Norwood, MA: ChristopherGordon.

Hartzler, M., & Henry, J. (1994). *Team fitness: A how-to manual for building a winning work team.* Milwaukee, WI: ASQC Quality Press.

Hertz-Lazarowitz, R., Kagan, S., Sharan, S., Slavin, R., & Webb, C. (Eds.). (1985). *Learning to cooperate: Cooperating to learn.* New York: Plenum.

Hill, S., & Eckert, P. (1995). *Leading communities of learners.* Adelaide, Australia: Management and Research Centre.

Hill, S., & Hancock, J. (1993). *Reading and writing communities.* Armadale, Australia: Portage & Main Press.

Hill, S., & Hill, T. (1990). *The collaborative classroom: A guide to cooperative learning.* Portsmouth, NH: Heinemann.

Hodgson, R., & Vogelphol, R. (2008). *Cooperative group work rubric.* Retrieved September 22, 2008, from http://www.lessonplanspage .com/SecretsOfTheUndergroundRailroadUnitCooperativeGroup WorkRubric4.htm

Hoffman, C., & Olson-Ness, J. (1996). *Tips and tools for trainers and teams.* Tacoma, WA: VISTA Associates.

Hythecker, V. I., Dansereau, D. F., & Rocklin, T. R. (1988). An analysis of the processes influencing the structured dyadic learning environment. *Educational Psychologist, 23,* 23–37.

Johnson, D. W., & Johnson, R. T. (1989). *Cooperation and competition: Theory and research.* Edina, MN: Interaction Book Company.

Johnson, D. W., & Johnson, R. T. (1991). *Cooperative learning.* Edina, MN: Interaction Book Company.

Johnson, D. W., & Johnson, R. T. (1997). *Learning to lead teams: Developing leadership skills.* Edina, MN: Interaction Book Company.

Johnson, D. W., Johnson, R. T., & Holubec, E. J. (1993). *Circles of learning* (4th ed.). Edina, MI: Interaction Book Company.

Jones, R. (1998). *3–2–1.* Retrieved August 28, 2006, from http://curry.edschool .virginia.edu/go/read quest/strat/321.html

Junior Reserve Officers Training Corps. (2006). *Lesson 5: Graphic organizers.* Retrieved August 28, 2006, from http://www.rotc.monroe.army .mil/JROTC/documents/Curriculum/Unit_3/u3c515.pdf

Kagan, S. (1992a). *Cooperative learning.* San Clemente, CA: Kagan Cooperative.

Kagan, S. (1992b). *Cooperative learning: Resources for teachers.* San Clemente, CA: Kagan Cooperative Learning.

Kim, A. H., Vaughn, S., Wanzek, J., & Wei, S. (2004). Graphic organizers and their effects on the reading comprehension of students with LD: A synthesis of research. *Journal of Learning Disabilities,* 37(2), 105–118.

Kintsch, W. (1974). *The representation of meaning in memory.* Hillsdale, NJ: Erlbaum.

Kulik, J., & Kulik, C. (1987, Spring). Effects of ability grouping on student achievement. *Equity and Excellence,* 23(1–2), 22–30.

Kuzmich, L. (1999). *School improvement planning using results.* Longmont, CO: CBOCES.

Kuzmich, L. (2003). *Scenario based learning.* Paper presented at Fall Conference for New Orleans Archdiocese, New Orleans, LA.

Kuzmich, L. (2007). *Redefining literacy in grades 7–12: Strategies for document, technological and quantitative literacy.* Rexford, NY: International Center for Leadership in Education.

Kuzmich, L. (2008). *Inspiring innovation.* Paper presented at Spring Symposium, International Center for Leadership in Education, San Diego, CA.

Lipton, L., Humbard, C., & Wellman, B. (2001). *Mentoring matters: A practical guide to learning-focused relationships.* Sherman, CT: MiraVia, LLC.

Long, M. H., Brock, C., Crookes, G., Deicke, L., Potter, L., Zhang, S. (1984*).* *The effects of teachers' questioning patterns and wait-time on pupil participation in public high school classes in Hawaii for students of limited English proficiency* (Technical Report No. 1). Honolulu, HI: University of Hawaii.

Lyman, F., & McTighe, J. (2001). Cueing thinking in the classroom: The promise of theory-embedded tools. In A. L. Costa (Ed.), *Developing minds: A resources book for teaching thinking* (3rd ed., Chapter 61). Alexandria, VA: ASCD.

Manzo, A., Manzo, U., & Albee, J. (2002). iREAP: Improving reading, writing, and thinking in the wired classroom. *Journal of Adolescent & Adult Literacy, 46,* 42–47.

Marzano, R. (2004). *Building background knowledge for academic achievement.* Alexandria, VA: ASCD.

Marzano, R. J., Norford, J. S., Paynter, D. E., Gaddy, B. B., & Pickering, D. J. (Eds.). (2004). *A handbook for classroom instruction that works.* Alexandria, VA: ASCD.

Marzano, R., Pickering, D., & Pollack, J. (2001). *Classroom instruction that works research-based strategies for increasing student achievement.* Alexandria, Virginia: ASCD.

McVee, M. B., Dunsmore, K., & Gavelek, J. R. (2005). Schema theory revisited. *Review of Educational Research, 75*(4), 531–566.

Meyer, E., & Smith, L. Z. (1987). *The Practical Tutor.* NY:Oxford University Press.

Murphy, N. (1994). *Authentic assessment for the learning cycle model.* Columbus, OH: ERIC Clearinghouse for Science, Mathematics, and Environmental Education.

North Central Regional Educational Laboratory (NCREL). (2006). *KWL.* Retrieved August 28, 2006, from http://www.ncrel.org/sdrs/areas/issues/students/learning/lr2kwl.htm

Panksepp, J. (1998). *Affective neuroscience: The foundations of human and animal emotions.* New York: Oxford University Press.

Pauk, W. (2001). *How to study in college.* Boston: Houghton Mifflin Company.

Peterson, K., & Deal, T. (2002). *The shaping school culture fieldbook.* San Francisco, CA: Jossey-Bass.

Prince, G. (1970). *Synectics—The practice of creativity: A manual for dynamic group problem solving.* New York: Harper & Row.

Qin, Z., Johnson, D. W., & Johnson, R. T. (1995). Cooperative versus competitive efforts and problem solving, *Review of Educational Research, 65*(2), 129–143.

Reid, J. (2002). *Managing small group learning.* Newtown, Australia: Primary English Teaching Association.

Renzulli, J. S. (1994). *Schools for talent development: A practical plan for total school improvement.* Mansfield Center, CT: Creative Learning Press.

Resnick, L. (Ed.). (1997). *Discourse, tools, and reasoning: Essays on situated cognition from the North Atlantic Treaty Organization Scientific Affairs Division.* New York: Springer.

Robbins, P., Gregory, G., & Herndon, L. (2000). *Thinking inside the block: Schedule strategies for teaching in extended periods of time.* Thousand Oaks, CA: Corwin.

Roberts, S., & Pruitt, E. (2003). Schools as professional learning communities: collaborative activities and strategies for professional development. Thousand Oaks, CA: Corwin.

Robertson, L., & Kagan, S. (1992). *Cooperative learning.* San Clemente, CA: Kagan Cooperative.

Roukes, N. (1988). *Design synectics: Stimulating creativity in design.* Worchester, MA: Davis Puhns.

Rowe, M. B. (1974). Wait-time and rewards as instructional variables. *Journal of Research in Science Teaching, 11,* 81–94.

Rowe, M. B. (1987). Wait time: Slowing down may be a way of speeding up. *American Educator, 11,* 38–73.

Silver, H., Strong, R., & Perini, M. (1997). *Cooperative learning.* Ho-Ho-Kus, NJ: Thoughtful Education Press.

Slavin, R. (1994). *A practical guide to cooperative learning.* Boston, MA: Allyn & Bacon.

Taba, H. (1967). *Teacher's handbook for elementary social studies.* Reading, MA: Addison-Wesley.

Tan, G., Gallo, P., Jacobs, G., & Lee, C. (1999). *Using cooperative learning to integrate thinking and information technology in a content-based writing lesson.* Retrieved August 8, 1999, from http://iteslj.org/Techniques/Tan-Cooperative.html. Internet TESL Journal, Vol. V. No. 8, August 1999.

van Dijk, T. A. (1980). *Macrostructures.* Hillsdale, NJ: Erlbaum.

Vantage Learning. (2007). *An interview with Dr. Douglas Reeves, founder of the Leadership and Learning Center.* Retrieved May 11, 2009, from http://www.vantagelearning.com/school/research/reeves_interview.html

Vaughan, J., & Estes, T. (1986). *Reading and reasoning beyond the primary grades.* Needham Heights, MA: Allyn & Bacon.

Wald, M., & Castleberry, P. (2000). *Educators as learners: Creating a professional learning community in your school.* Alexandria, VA: ASCD.

Webb, N. M. (1989). Peer interaction and learning in small groups. *International Journal of Educational Research, 13,* 21–39.

Wolfe, P., & Brandt, R. (1998). What do we know from brain research? *Educational Leadership, 56*(3), 8–13.

Zike, D. (1992). *Big book of books and activities.* San Antonio, TX: Dinah-Might Adventures, LP.

Zygouris-Coe, V., Wiggins, M. B., & Smith, L. H. (2004). Engaging students with text: The 3–2-1 strategy. *The Reading Teacher, 58,* 381–384.

Index

CORWIN
A SAGE Company

The Corwin logo—a raven striding across an open book—represents the union of courage and learning. Corwin is committed to improving education for all learners by publishing books and other professional development resources for those serving the field of PreK–12 education. By providing practical, hands-on materials, Corwin continues to carry out the promise of its motto: **"Helping Educators Do Their Work Better."**

DATE DUE

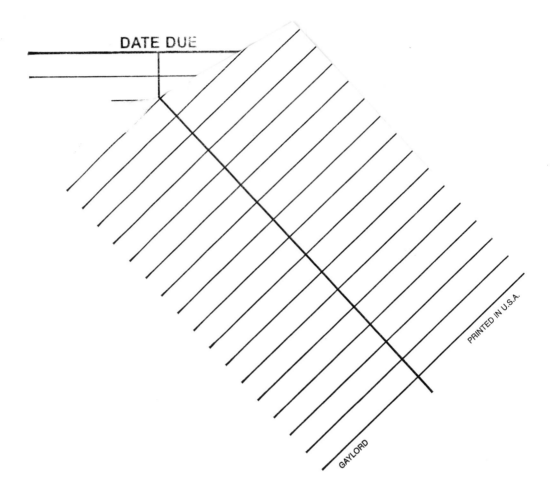

GAYLORD

PRINTED IN U.S.A.